Frommer's™

W9-ARX-892

Copenhagen
day BY day™
1st Edition

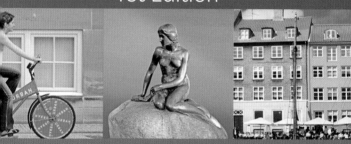

by Sasha Heseltine

WILEY

A John Wiley and Sons, Ltd, Publication

Contents

UK Publisher: Sally Smith
Executive Project Editor: Daniel Mersey
Commissioning Editor: Fiona Quinn
Content Editor: Erica Peters
Development Editor: Jill Emeny
Photo Research: Jill Emeny
Cartography: Tom Blatchard

Wiley also publishes its books in a variety of electronic formats. Some content that appears in print may not be available in electronic books.

British Library Cataloguing in Publication Data
A catalogue record for this book is available from the British Library

ISBN: 978-0-470-69953-9
Typeset by Wiley Indianapolis Composition Services

Printed and bound in China by RR Donnelley

5 4 3 2 1

A Note from the Editorial Director

Organizing your time. That's what this guide is all about.

Other guides give you long lists of things to see and do and then expect you to fit the pieces together. The Day by Day guides are different. These guides tell you the best of everything, and then they show you how to see it *in the smartest, most time-efficient way*. Our authors have designed detailed itineraries organized by time, neighborhood, or special interest. And each tour comes with a bulleted map that takes you from stop to stop.

Hoping to tour the best in modern architecture, discover museum highlights, and see some fantastic art? Fancy a trip to the setting of Shakespeare's *Hamlet* or a tour round historic palaces? Whatever your interest or schedule, the Day by Days give you the smartest routes to follow. Not only do we take you to the top attractions, hotels, and restaurants, but we also help you access those special moments that locals get to experience—those "finds" that turn tourists into travelers.

The Day by Days are also your top choice if you're looking for one complete guide for all your travel needs. The best hotels and restaurants for every budget, the greatest shopping values, the wildest nightlife—it's all here.

Why should you trust our judgment? Because our authors personally visit each place they write about. They're an independent lot who say what they think and would never include places they wouldn't recommend to their best friends. They're also open to suggestions from readers. If you'd like to contact them, please send your comments our way at feedback@frommers.com, and we'll pass them on.

Enjoy your Day by Day guide—the most helpful travel companion you can buy. And have the trip of a lifetime.

Warm regards,

Kelly Regan

Kelly Regan, Editorial Director
Frommer's Travel Guides

About the Author

Sasha Heseltine has been in travel publishing as both writer and editor for many years, starting out at Dorling Kindersley in London. She worked on mini-guides for Berlitz before heading for the West Country to Compass Maps, where she produced 48 InsideOut map-guides to cities across the world. She now works as a freelancer and recently edited the Frommer's With Your Family guides to Florida, Naples, and Tuscany & Umbria, as well as the Day by Day guide to Istanbul. She has also written the *Frommer's Milan & the Lakes Day by Day* guide.

Acknowledgments

A big thank you to Fiona for thinking of me and all her patience. Many thanks to Henrik Thierlein and Ana Lia Bright at Visit Copenhagen, as well as Marcus Nardy from the Hotel D'Angleterre for making me laugh. And love to George, as ever.

An Additional Note

Please be advised that travel information is subject to change at any time—and this is especially true of prices. We therefore suggest that you write or call ahead for confirmation when making your travel plans. The authors, editors, and publisher cannot be held responsible for the experiences of readers while traveling. Your safety is important to us, however, so we encourage you to stay alert and be aware of your surroundings.

Star Ratings, Icons & Abbreviations

Every hotel, restaurant, and attraction listing in this guide has been ranked for quality, value, service, amenities, and special features using a **star-rating system.** Hotels, restaurants, attractions, shopping, and nightlife are rated on a scale of zero stars (recommended) to three stars (exceptional). In addition to the star-rating system, we also use a **kids** icon to point out the best bets for families. Within each tour, we recommend cafes, bars, or restaurants where you can take a break. Each of these stops appears in a shaded box marked with a coffee-cup-shaped bullet ☕.

The following **abbreviations** are used for credit cards:

AE	American Express	DISC	Discover	V	Visa
DC	Diners Club	MC	MasterCard		

Frommers.com

Now that you have this guidebook to help you plan a great trip, visit our web-site at **www.frommers.com** for additional travel information on more than 4,000 destinations. We update features regularly to give you instant access to the most current trip-planning information available. At Frommers.com, you'll find scoops on the best airfares, lodging rates, and car rental bargains. You can even book your travel online through our reliable travel booking partners.

A Note on Prices

In the "Take a Break" and "Best Bets" sections of this book, we have used a system of dollar signs to show a range of costs for 1 night in a hotel (the price of a double-occupancy room) or the cost of an entree at a restaurant. Use the following table to decipher the dollar signs:

Cost	Hotels	Restaurants
$	under $100	under $10
$$	$100–$200	$10–$20
$$$	$200–$300	$20–$30
$$$$	$300–$400	$30–$40
$$$$$	over $400	over $40

An Invitation to the Reader

In researching this book, we discovered many wonderful places—hotels, restaurants, shops, and more. We're sure you'll find others. Please tell us about them, so we can share the information with your fellow travelers in upcoming editions. If you were disappointed with a recommendation, we'd love to know that, too. Please write to:

Frommer's Copenhagen, Day by Day, 1st Edition
Wiley Publishing, Inc. • 111 River St. • Hoboken, NJ 07030-5774

17 Favorite
Moments

17 Favorite Moments

NYHOLM

Dannebrog Samsøes Allé

SYDHAVNEN

HOLMEN

Elvigsmestervej

Arsenaløen

Kastellet

Larsens Plads

CHRISTIANSHAVN

Esplanaden

Grønningen

Bredgade

Store Kongensgade

Skt. Annæ Plads

Borgergade

Kongens Nytorv

Dronningens Tværgade

Christians Brygge

Sølvgade

Kongens Have

Børsgade

Knippelsbro

Øster Voldgade

Øster Farimagsgade

Frederiksborggade

Købmagergade

Strøget

Amagertorv

Rådhusstræde

Frederiksholms Kanal

Botanisk Have

Gothersgade

Nørregade

THE LATIN QUARTER

Frederiksberggade

Øster Søgade

Ørsteds Parken

Vester Voldgade

Nørre Voldgade

Vester Farimagsgade

Tivoli

Bernstorffsgade

Ostre Anlæg

Sortedams Sø

Dronning Louises Bro

Nørre Farimagsgade

Nørrebro

Peblinge Sø

Gyldenløvesgade

Kampmannsgade

Skt. Jørgens Sø

Central Station

Fælledvej

VESTERBRO

Gammel Kongevej

Vesterbrogade

Copenhagen is the perfect holiday destination—a compact city that is easy to navigate, and bursting with royal palaces, innovative design museums, great shops, and vast green parks to kick back in. Add to that mix the hip and plentiful bars, cafés, and restaurants and entertaining daytrips and you have an enticing package. Here are some of my favorite things to do in the booming Danish capital and environs.

1 **Lunching canal-side in the sun at Nyhavn;** preferably at Cap Horn for its excellent organic dishes and superb langoustines! If it's cold, wrap up in a blanket and huddle under one of the outside heaters. *See p 96.*

2 **Kicking back with a book in Kongelige Bibliotek Haven** (King's Library Gardens) on a bench just by the fountain. Perfect for reflecting on your visit to the Danske Jødisk Museum (Danish Jewish Museum). *See p 19.*

3 **Walking off a Nyhavn lunch along Langelinie** on a Sunday afternoon to admire the Lille Havfrue (Little Mermaid, see p 59) and her less attractive friend, the Mutant Mermaid, in Østbassin. *See p 17.*

4 **Savoring a long and leisurely lunch** at my favorite and very atmospheric Copenhagen restaurant, Café Petersborg. Try the herring, pickled and marinated! *See p 94.*

A visit to the Little Mermaid.

Tivoli Pagoda.

5 **Getting a taste for Danish decorative arts** at the Kunstindustrimuseet. Take time to walk around the industrial designs and functionalist furniture in the modern collections. *See p 16.*

6 **Zooming at high speed around the Tivoli roller coasters** and afterwards eating a hot dog from one of the food stalls. *See p 10.*

7 **Joining the elegant ladies of Frederiksberg** (see p 52) for delicately constructed 'smushi' (a mixture of sushi and smørrebrød) at the Royal Café (see p 100) and afterwards a trip around the Royal Copenhagen flagship store to buy the famous blue-and-white china. See p 43.

8 Exploring the canals by boat; cruise by some of Copenhagen's most famous sights and get your bearings in the city. *See p 7.*

9 Cycling around the city because there is so little traffic in Copenhagen; much of the center is pedestrianized and there are cycle lanes on the majority of roads. *See p 85.*

10 Shopping in Strædet; the cobbled streets and vintage and antique stores of Læderstræde and Kompagnistræde are ideal for bargain hunters. *See p 9.*

11 Admiring the vast sculpture collections at Ny Carlsberg Glyptotek and strolling among the palms and classical statuary of the domed Winter Garden. *See p 14.*

12 Walking around the battlements at Kronborg Slot (castle, see p 146) on its wild and remote headland in the north of Zealand, before settling in for a vast plate of pasta at Peccati di Gola on the edge of Helsingør's old town. *See p 147.*

13 Catching sight of the glittering waters of the Øresund from the glass-walled galleries at Louisiana Museum of Modern Art and walking in the rolling grounds after pleasantly overdosing on contemporary art. *See p 154.*

14 Watching the sun rise over Helsingborg in Sweden from the Marienlyst Hotel (see p 134) in Helsingør after a stormy night. *See p 134.*

15 Buying rough-hewn bread and organic picnic supplies from Emmery's, a store with several branches throughout Copenhagen. Those delicious foodie smells! *See p 80.*

16 Making a fuss of the handsome Jutland horses in the stables at the Carlsberg Visitors Centre (see p 50) and afterwards enjoying a glass of chilled lager at The Jacobsen Brewhouse. *See p 107.*

17 Getting down to a spot of rowing on the fjord in a replica longboat at Roskilde Viking Ship Museum. Afterwards visit the original longboats, dating from the 11th century. *See p 138.* ●

The ramparts at Kronborg Slot.

1

The Best
Full-Day Tours

The Best in One Day

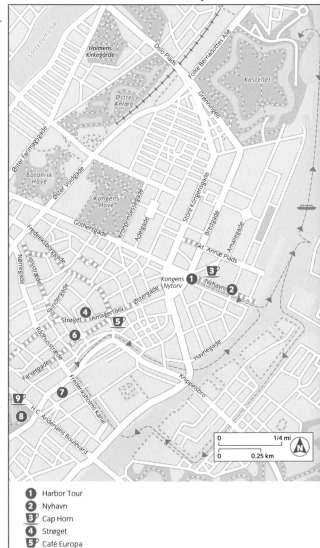

1 Harbor Tour
2 Nyhavn
3 Cap Horn
4 Strøget
5 Café Europa
6 Strædet
7 Nationalmuseet
8 Tivoli
9 Café Ketchup

Time to immerse yourself in romantic, chic Copenhagen. This city is about more than fabulous art collections and serious museums, although it has its fair share. Take to the cobbled streets to get right to its laid-back heart. See the city from the sea on a harbor trip and savor the casual vibe in the restaurants of Nyhavn before discovering the shopping streets of the old town and taking a tour of Danish history in Copenhagen's biggest museum. Wind up your day at the iconic pleasure gardens of Tivoli to scream around roller coasters and feast on the finest Danish cuisine. START: **Kongens Nytorv.**

1 ★★★ kids **Harbor Tour.** Boat tours leave half hourly from the top of Nyhavn Canal and I recommend taking one to get your bearings and understand how the city has developed from its medieval infancy to the cutting-edge destination of today. Take the Red Line boat trip to the north of the harbor and sit at the front of the boat if you want to catch the English commentary. As you leave Nyhavn, look left for the much-celebrated **Det Kongelige Teater Skuespilhuset** (Royal Danish Playhouse, see p 122), opened in February 2008. Right across the water you'll spy the innovative Opera House (see p 119), with a curving four-story foyer and cantilevered roof, floating on its man-made island. On the left and just downstream from the Queen's palace at Amalienborg (see p 15) there's a photo opportunity at the Little Mermaid (see p 59), who sits on an empty shoreline gazing wistfully out to sea. On the return journey through the canals of Christianshavn (see p 63) get cameras ready for the gold-topped Vor Frelsers Kirke, which appears on the left (see p 64), and the sparkling Den Sorte Diamant (Black Diamond), housing part of Denmark's royal library (see p 30), which looms up as you turn out of Christianshavn Canal. Before returning to Nyhavn, the boat putters around the islet of Slotsholmen (see p 19), site of Copenhagen's first palace, built by Bishop Absalon (see p 19), who founded the city in 1167AD. ⏱ *1 hr. DFDS Canal*

Tours, Nyhavn 1433 (at head of canal). ☎ *+45 3296 3000. www.canal tours.com. Book in advance at Copenhagen Tourist Office, Vesterbrogade 4a.* ☎ *+45 7022 2442. www.visit copenhagen.com. Tickets 60DKK adults, 30DKK kids; 20% discount with Copenhagen Card (see p 8). Daily Mar 15–June 27 & Aug 25–Oct 21 9.30am–5pm; June 28–Aug 24 9.30am–7pm; Oct 22–Dec 21 10.15am–3.15pm. Departures every 30 mins except Oct 22– Dec 21, when trips leave at 10.15am, 11.30am, 12.45pm, 2pm & 3.15pm. Closed: Dec 22–Mar 14. Metro: Kongens Nytorv.*

2 ★★★ kids **Nyhavn.** Built in the 17th century to connect Copenhagen to the sea, Nyhavn is bisected by its canal and lined with crooked, brightly

Reflection of passing tour boats in the glass of the Black Diamond.

Save Money with a CPH Card

The Copenhagen Card: don't go out without it. This brilliantly conceived card gives free entrance to 63 museums (all the major ones, but not Tivoli or Roskilde Viking Ship Museum, see p 138) plus free travel on public transport (bus, metro, train, and harbor bus, see p 162) throughout Copenhagen and beyond. At the time of writing, a 24-hour CPH Card cost 209DKK, a 72-hour card 439DKK. When you are ready to use your card, sign and date it, and write in your starting time; it's valid from that point. Two children go free with one adult card. Buy the card online (www.visitcopenhagen.com), from the tourist office at Vesterbrogade 4a (☎ +45 7022 2442), or at the airport.

painted gabled houses. Once home to sailors and dockworkers, the street was notorious for seedy drinking dens. Today the crowds and venues are still here but they've both gone up-market. Welcoming cafés, bars, and restaurants offer cold beers and (mostly) excellent local dishes at tables spilling into the street. Choose somewhere to eat and settle down to watch the world go by—my preferences are Cap Horn (see below), Leonore Christiane (see p 99), and **SARS Kommandøren** (see p 100) for quality seafood and organic meat dishes. ⏱ *45 min. Nyhavn. Metro: Kongens Nytorv.*

3 ★★ **Cap Horn.** My first choice at Nyhavn for a leisurely lunch of fresh langoustines and thinly sliced beef with pickles. If the sun is shining, grab a table in the street-side bar and order a chilled dark lager. *See p 96. Nyhavn 15. ☎ +45 3314 5614. www.sars.dk. $$.*

4 ★★★ **Strøget.** Europe's longest pedestrianized shopping street runs 1.8 km from Kongens Nytorv down to the Rådhuspladsen, moving progressively downmarket as it goes. At the top end, have

credit cards at the ready for Cartier, Gucci, Mulberry, and Chanel as well as department store Illum (see p 77), beloved of wealthy Copenhagen matrons, and its delightful sidekick design emporium, Illums Bolighus (see p 78), where I enjoy seeing the color-coordinated displays. Acclaimed silversmith Georg Jensen's flagship store (see p 82) is here too, next door to Royal Copenhagen (see p 76), doing a roaring trade in its famous blue-and-white pottery. Among the high-street names popping up further down Strøget (Accessorize, H&M), Bodum stands out for selling quality Danish

Designerware in Illums Bolighus.

design at sensible prices. ⏲ 1½ hr. *Strøget. Metro: Kongens Nytorv. Short stroll from Nyhavn.*

Eskimo boots at the Nationalmuseet.

5 ★★ kids **Café Europa.** At the heart of Strøget, Copenhagen's famous pedestrianized shopping street, **Café Europa** boasts an award-winning barlista (coffee expert) and a selection of sinful teatime cakes. See p 93. *Amagertorv 1.* ☎ *+45 3314 2889. $.*

6 ★★★ **Strædet.** Discover the romantic tangle of narrow cobbled streets to the south of Strøget. You couldn't do better for hip boutiques, dusty old vinyl shops, and crowded cafés overflowing with students. Look out for Læderstræde and Kompagnistræde, lined with basement antique shops selling silverware, porcelain, and delicate glass (not many bargains to be found here). These shops are found on the streets running parallel to the left of Strøget as you head towards Rådhuspladsen. ⏲ 1 hr. Latin Quarter. Metro: Kongens Nytorv. Stroll from Strøget.

7 ★★ kids **Nationalmuseet (National Museum).** It's time for a whistle-stop tour of Danish history at the National Museum, housed in an 18th-century palace with a new atrium just off Rådhuspladsen. The collection is broken down into themes (ethnographic, coins and medals, Middle Ages and Renaissance, Prince's Palace) but don't try to see too much in one go; the collection is vast and navigating around it is time-consuming. I advise you to choose one of several 60-minute audio-guides (find near the ticket desk) to steer you through the highlights. If you're travelling *en famille*, there's an interactive children's museum to spark little imaginations (see p 34). Worth a visit are the ethnographic collections (first floor, rooms 151–172) where you can see an Inuit snow suit, an eerily beautiful Edo period golden screen decorated with frolicking horses, and a collection of Samurai costumes. Tour the state rooms of 1743, complete with fine Flemish tapestries (rooms 127–134 on the first floor) and don't

Monday Closing

Don't get caught out: many museums and attractions in Copenhagen close on Monday, including most of those mentioned in this chapter. There's still lots to do; take a harbor trip past the Little Mermaid, enjoy *smørrebrød* (open sandwiches—they're so much more enticing than they sound) overlooking the canal at Nyhavn, wander around Christianshavn (see p 63), or visit the Viking Ship Museum at Roskilde (see p 138).

Slotsholmen Museums

After Nyhavn, if you don't want to walk any further or the kids don't want to go shopping, you can always stop off on the island of Slotsholmen, where there are seven museums, including the Royal Reception Rooms (see p 39), **Ruinerne af Absalons** (Absalon's Ruins, see p 19), **Daniel Libeskind's Danske Jødisk Museum** (Danish Jewish Museum, see p 19), **Tøjhusmuseet** (Royal Danish Arsenal Museum, see p 35), **Kongelige Bibliotek** (Royal Library, see p 19). For the **Thorvaldsens Museum**, showcasing one man's obsession with sculpture, and **Teatermuseet**, see p 39.

miss the mystical Iron Age Gundestrop Cauldron, decorated with carved Celtic warriors and dogs, the symbol of death, just off the atrium. ⏲ *1 hr. Frederiksholms Kanal 12.* ☎ *+45 3313 4411. www.national museet.dk. Free admission. Tues–Sun 10am–5pm. Closed Dec 24–25, 31. Bus 6a. 10-min. walk from Strædet.*

8 ★★★ **kids** **Tivoli.** Bewitching Tivoli weaves its magic after dark, when all its pavilions, pagodas, and follies, intricately landscaped boating lakes and gardens are brightly floodlit. Founded in 1843, the pleasure

Fairy lights in Tivoli at night.

gardens are as Danish as bacon and maintain a sweetly old-fashioned appeal, pulling daily crowds by the thousand. You'll find 25 rides to choose from; for spine-tingling chills, head to the Golden Tower, with its high-velocity vertical drop of 63m, then get inverted hurtling at 77mph (125kph) around the madcap Demon roller coaster. There are also many gentle attractions specially aimed at young kids (see p 33). But there's so much more to Tivoli than fairground rides. The concert hall (see p 118) is home to the Tivoli Symphony Orchestra and a seasonal program of cultural events. Jazz and rock concerts take place in the ornate Glass Hall Theatre (see p 118) and on the open-air stage, while mime fans love the nightly shows at the Pantomime Theatre (see p 116). Food and drink options are endless, whatever your budget. Grab a hot dog on the hoof, sink a pint of lager in the Beer Garden, or sit down for a formal dinner in one of Tivoli's pricey restaurants (see The Best Dining). ⏲ *3 hrs. Vesterbrogade 3.* ☎ *+45 3313 4411. www.tivoli.dk. Admission 85DKK, 45DKK children aged 3–11. Multi-ride tickets 200DKK, 160DKK kids 3–11. Apr 17–Dec 30 Sun–Thur 10am–10pm; Fri–Sat 10am–11pm. Closed Jan–mid-Apr. Bus 2A, 5A, 15. 10-min walk from Nationalmuseet.*

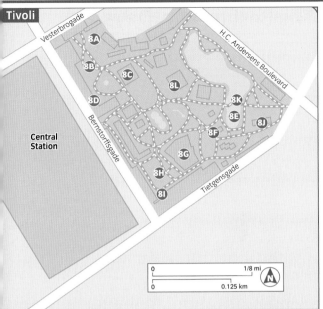

Tivoli

8A ★★★ kids **Pantomime-teatret**, The Chinese pavilion (see p 117) to the left of the main entrance stages nightly performances of mime and panto. Opposite is the 8B ★ **Promenade Pavilion**, home to the Tivoli Promenade Orchestra. There's rock music at the 8C ★★ **Plænen (Open-air Stage Tivoli)**, where local kids hang around looking for action (see p 120).To your right, 8D ★★★ **Nimb Palace** has trendy restaurant, bar, and hotel (see p 132). Walk to the ornamental lake and on the left is 8E ★★★ kids **Tivoli Lake**, with Dragon Boats (see p 33) for children. Take toddlers on the 8F ★★ kids **Trolley Bus** to explore the rest of the gardens—it stops by the Illums Bolighus store (see p 78) on your left.

Straight ahead the 8G ★★ **Tivoli Concert Hall** provides music by the resident symphony orchestra (see p 118) and mainstream concerts. Around the hall to the right are 8H ★★★ kids **Rides** including bumper cars, Nautilus and the Star Flyer for the brave (see p 33).The 8I ★★ kids **Amusement Arcade** provides old-fashioned fun, and candy floss. A scary 8J kids **Demon Roller Coaster**, has high-speed inversions, and the Golden Tower boasts unbearable drops (see p 10). Cross the ★ **Wooden bridge** over the floodlit lake and follow the shore around to 8K ★ kids the **Tivoli**

9 ★★★ **Café Ketchup.** The 40+ food outlets in Tivoli range from hot dog stands to haute cuisine. Ketchup is delightful inside and has an excellent Danish fusion menu. I highly recommend the Sunday brunch. See p 94. *Tivoli. Vesterbrogade 3.* ☎ *45 3375 0755. www.cafeketchup tivoli.dk. $$$.*

The Best in Two Days

Today's the day to ingest a little more culture. You'll see a rare and immense collection of antiquities and the very best of Danish decorative arts. Between times, visit the Royal Family at home and introduce your kids to the fairy-tale world of Hans Christian Andersen. There's a chance to stretch your legs along the seafront and the promise of a slap-up supper to round off your day.

1 ★ **kids** **The Wonderful World of Hans Christian Andersen.** If you are traveling with young kids or have a keen interest in the works of Denmark's favorite storyteller, this is a good option to start the morning, with a series of tableaux illustrating Andersen's fairy-cum-morality tales, plus letters, newspaper clippings, and photographs to appeal to older visitors. 🕐 *1 hr. Rådhuspladsen 57.* ☎ *+45 3232 3131. www.hcandersen. com. Admission 67DKK, 54DKK kids 11–14, 34DKK kids 4–10, free with Copenhagen Card. Jan 2–June 14 & Sept 1–Dec 31 Sun–Thurs 10am–6pm; Fri–Sat 10am–8pm; June 15–Aug 31 daily 10am–8pm. Closed Dec 24–25 & 31, Jan 1. Bus 10, 12, 14, 26, 29, 33, 48, 67, 68, 89, 2A, 5A, 6A, 173E.*

2 ★ **Rådhus & Astronomical Clock.** If whimsical fairy stories are not your thing, take a detour to the monumental architecture of the Rådhus (town hall), which dominates the eastern end of its busy square. Built at the turn of the 20th century by Martin Nyrop (1849–1921), Scandinavia's leading romantic architect, who also designed the Eliaskirken in Vesterbro. Influenced by the Palazzo Pubblico in Siena, the city hall is studded with carvings of mythical creatures and its 106m tower gives great views over the city and Tivoli (see p 10). Jens Olsen's World Clock is hidden away in a room off the main foyer. Completed in 1955, it has 14,000 moving parts, perfectly exhibited in a double-sided glass case.

Astronomical clock in the Rådhus.

Thumbelina at The Wonderful World of Hans Christian Andersen.

There are guided tours of the massive mock-Gothic city halls and trips up the tower at 12pm. ⏱ *30 min. Rådhuspladsen 1.* ☎ *+45 3366 7032. www.kk.dk. Admission: (tower) 20DKK; (clock) 10DKK, 5DKK kids, free with Copenhagen Card. Guided tours 30DKK. Guided tours in English: Mon–Fri 3pm; Sat 10am. Tower tours Mon–Fri 12pm. Bus 10, 12, 14, 26, 29, 33, 48, 67, 68, 89, 2A, 5A, 6A, 173E.*

❸ ★★★ NY Carlsberg Glyptotek (Carlsberg Collection). Cross over Hans Christian Andersen Boulevard to an unsurpassable collection of antiquities and 19th-century French and Danish paintings donated to Copenhagen in 1897 by scions of the Carlsberg brewing dynasty (see p 50). The ancient sculptures are gathered from Egypt, Greece, and Rome and are laid out in two light-filled neoclassical galleries built around a charming sculpture-and-plant-filled courtyard garden. Make a point of seeing the gilded sarcophagus of Aurelia Kyrelia (300AD), the impassive head of Roman goddess Juno (she's had a nose job) and the evocative Greek statue of an actress holding the head of Dionysus, dating from 200AD. Helge Carlsberg's collection of Danish and French art hangs well in local architect Henning Larsen's minimalist three-story gallery extension. Highlights include Van Gogh's stark 1889 *Landscape from Saint-Remy*, several of Gauguin's Tahitian women, and a series of Degas's ballet-dancer bronzes. There's a delicious but expensive café in the palm-filled Winter Garden (see p 93). ⏱ *2 hrs. Dantes Plads 7.* ☎ *+45 3341 8141. www.glyptotek. dk. Admission 50DKK adults, free for kids under 18, free with Copenhagen Card. Tues–Sun 10am–4pm. Closed every Mon, Jan 1, June 5, Dec 24–25. Bus 1a, 2a, 10, 12, 14, 15, 26, 29, 33, 48, 67, 68, 89, 2A, 5A, 6A, 173E.*

The Egyptian Room in NY Carlsberg Glyptotek.

The Dome inside the Marmorkirken.

2-min walk across Rådhuspladsen from Wonderful Word of Hans Christian Andersen.

4 ★★★ **Café à Porta.** All Belle Epoque decoration, dark and moody, this is an expensive but glamorous pit stop for lunch and is popular in the evening for steak and chips. See p 94. *Kongens Nytorv 17.* ☎ *+45 3311 0305. www.cafeaporta.dk. $$$.*

5 ★★ **Amalienborgmuseet (Amalienborg Museum).** Walk off lunch to the rococo palaces of the Amalienborg complex, built in the 1750s by Nicolas Eigtved (1701–1754, who also played a role in building the palace at Christiansborg), and still used by the Royal Family today. With your back to the imperious equestrian statue of Frederik V, look towards the dome of the Marmorkirken (see p 16). The palace immediately to the left serves as luxury accommodation for visiting diplomats; there are guided tours between June and September. The next palace on the left is the winter home of the present Queen, Margrethe II. Crown Prince Frederik and his Tasmanian-born wife Princess Mary will move in 2010 to the fourth palace but for now are based in the first palace on the right. This is partly open to the public; a series of royal apartments house royal jewels, paintings, and costumes, plus fascinating family portraits. A recreation of Frederik VIII's opulent study from 1869 is dominated by a very non-PC polar bear skin. ⏱ *1 hr. Christian VIII's Palace.* ☎ *+45 3315 3286. www.amalienborgmuseet.dk. Admission 50DKK, 40DKK students, 30DKK over 65, 15DKK kids 5–14, free with*

Keep the Change

Most museums won't allow bags and backpacks to be taken into the galleries: all baggage has to be deposited in lockers before entry so I made sure to carry 10 and 20DKK coins with me to operate the lockers. The coins are refundable when you reclaim your belongings.

Copenhagen Card. Jan 2–Apr 30 & Nov 1–Dec 18 Tues–Sun 11am–4pm; May 1–Oct 31 daily 10am–4pm. Closed Mon, Jan 2–Apr 30 & Nov 1–Dec 18. Bus 1A, 15, 20E.

6 ★ **Marmorkirken (Marble Church).** Properly called Frederiks Kirke and designed as part of the Amalienborg palace complex (see p 15) in the 1750s, this Baroque church was eventually inaugurated in 1894. The 31m dome was to be clad in marble (hence its nickname), but, alas, the budget didn't stretch to that. Still, they made up for it inside; the decorative dome is gilded and smothered with representations of the prophets and cherubim. Choral concerts are held here in summer. ⏱ *30 min. Frederiksgade 4.* ☎ *+45 3315 0144. www.marmorkirken.dk. Free admission. Mon, Tues & Thu 10am–5pm; Wed 10am–6pm; Fri–Sun 12pm–5pm. Bus 1A, 15, 20E. 5-min. walk from Amalienborgmuseet.*

7 ★★★ **kids Kunstindustrimuseet (Danish Museum of Art and Design).** This impressive collection of decorative arts is in a former hospital backing on to tranquil lawns. Where else can you find blue-patterned drinking cups and tulip vases from the Golden Age of the Dutch and Danish guilds, Chinese and Japanese ceramics, embroidery, and avant-garde contemporary Danish design under the same roof? The late, great Arne Jacobsen and Scotland's Charles Rennie Mackintosh are given floor space alongside an extensive lace collection, temporary exhibitions and the Design Studio, where kids can handle ceramics and other crafts. My only complaint is that English labeling is sparse. ⏱ *2 hrs. Bredgade 68.* ☎ *+45 3318 5650. www.kunstindustrimuseet.dk. Admission 50DKK, 35DKK students & over 65s, free kids under 18, free with Copenhagen Card. Tues–Sun 11am–5pm. Closed Mon, Dec 24–25, Jan 1. Metro: Kongens Nytorv. 5-min. walk from Marmokirken.*

8 ★ **kids Kastellet.** Built by Christian IV in 1626 as a star-shaped fortress to strengthen the city walls, Kastellet suffered damage during

Surprisingly tiny, the Little Mermaid.

Dine in Danish style at Café Petersborg.

both the Swedish Siege of Copenhagen (1658–1660) and by the British in 1807 during the Napoleonic Wars. Today the buildings inside the fortress are occupied by the army although the public can still enjoy a stroll outside and watch swans swim about the moat. Langelinie (see below) starts from here. ⏱ *45 min. Churchilparken.* ☎ *+45 3311 2233. Admission free. Metro: Kongens Nytorv. 5-min walk from Kunstindustrimuseet.*

⑨ ★ kids Langelinie. Join Copenhageners on an afternoon's promenade along Langelinie (turn right and then left from the Kunstindustrimuseet, see p 16) to follow the shoreline along Øresund. The bronze statue of mythical Gefion ploughing up land to create Denmark looms up next to the 17th-century ramparts of the Kastellet (see above). A couple of hundred meters along Langelinie, Edvard Eriksen's iconic *Little Mermaid* (see

p 59) has been perched on her rocky island since 1913. Carry on up Langelinie Quay to the cruise-liner port and turn left into Østbassin for another intriguing pile of stones with a mermaid atop. Dubbed the *Mutant Mermaid,* this sculpture is twisted like a figure in a Mannerist painting and sits opposite a sinister group sculpture called *Paradise Genetically Altered,* a distorted vision of the Holy Family; both are by anarchic artist Bjørn Nørgaard. From here walk back to Bredgade for dinner or catch the number 26 bus into the city center. ⏱ *15 min. Bus 26. 1-hr round walk to and from to Bredgade.*

⑩ ★★★ Café Petersborg. A real treat in atmospheric basement premises, serving the best herring in town, presented three ways: marinated, pickled, or curried. See p 94. *Bredgade 76.* ☎ *+45 3312 5016. www.cafe-petersborg.dk. $$.*

The Best in Three Days

1. Café Diamanten
2. Museums at Slotsholmen
3. Ruinerne af Absalons
4. Danske Jødisk Museum
5. Rundetårn
6. Købmagergade
7. Rosenborg Slot
8. Statens Museum for Kunst
9. Karen Blixen Museum
10. Spicylicious

There's more art and history on offer today as well as the chance to peer across the Copenhagen skyline—obviously you will see more if you choose a clear day. Take a look at Slotsholmen, the island power-base of Danish politics for a thousand years, and visit a couple of unusual museums, one up the coast near the marina in Rungsted. Wear a pair of comfy shoes for walking along Copenhagen's cobbled streets! START: **Rådhuspladsen**.

1 Café Diamanten. Stop off for a mid-morning frothy *café au lait* and chocolate croissant. If you are feeling slothful, indulge in a hearty and heavy full Danish breakfast. *Gammel Strand 50.* ☎ *+45 3393 5545. www.cafediamanten.dk. $.*

2 Museums at Slotsholmen. The tiny island of **Slotsholmen** was the site of Bishop Absalon's Copenhagen in the 12th century and subsequent home to the Danish Royal Family in a series of ever-more flamboyant palaces. Today it houses the Danish Parliament in Christiansborg Palace (see p 39), a grand neoclassical church and seven diverse museums. The two described below are my recommendations, for their unusual content, but see p 10 for other options.

3 ★★★ kids Ruinerne af Absalons (Absalon's Ruins). The foundations of Absalon's castle lie below Christiansborg Palace in an atmospheric little museum; entry is through the arched front gateway. See granite pillars from the chapel, remains of the castle's protective double walls, and the ruins of Absalon's Secret—a coy euphemism for the medieval bathrooms! ⏱ *45 min. Kongeporten.*

☎ *+45 3392 6492. www.ses.dk/ruins. Admission 40DKK, 30DKK students and over 65s, kids under 16 free, free with Copenhagen Card. Daily May–Sept 10am–4pm; Oct–Apr Tues–Sun 10am–4pm. Metro: Kongens Nytorv. 5-min walk from Gammel Strand.*

4 ★★ Danske Jødisk Museum (Danish Jewish Museum). Tucked away in a corner of the Kongelige Bibliotek (Royal Library), this little museum is worth a visit just to experience the startling slopes and angles of Daniel Libeskind's extraordinary design. The collection tells the 400-year-old story of Jewish life in Denmark through a series of interactive and clearly labeled exhibits, including ornate Chanukah candlesticks and illuminated Torah manuscripts. The tranquil, fountain-filled garden outside is my secret spot to take a few moments out. ⏱ *45 min. Proviantpassagen 6.* ☎ *+45 3311 2218. www.jewmus.dk. Admission 40DKK, 30DKK students and over 65s, free for kids under 16, free with Copenhagen Card. Sept 1–May 31 Tues–Fri 1pm–4pm; Sat–Sun 12pm–5pm; June 1–Aug 31 Tues–Sun 10am–5pm. Closed Mon. Metro: Kongens Nytorv. 5-min walk from Gammel Strand.*

Statue of King Frederik VII outside Christiansborg Palace.

Entrance to the Jewish Museum on Slotsholmen.

5 ★★★ kids **Rundetårn (Round Tower).** Commissioned in 1642 by King Christian IV as an observatory for astronomer Tycho Brahe, the Rundetårn now hosts art exhibitions and concerts. Wend your way up the circular internal ramp to the top for the best views across Copenhagen's Latin Quarter (see p 60). At 35m high, you'll see the Øresund, the rides of Tivoli, and the tower of Christiansborg Palace (see p 39) as Copenhagen stretches into the distance. ⏱ *45 min. Købmagergade 52a.* ☎ *+45 3373 0373.* www. rundetaarn.dk. *Admission 25DKK,*

The Rundetårn on an icy winter's day.

15DKK kids 5–15, free with Copenhagen Card. Tower open daily Sept 21–May 20 10am–5pm; May 21–Sept 19 10am–8pm; Observatory open daily mid-Oct–mid-Mar 7pm–10pm; Jul 1–Aug 12 Sun 1pm–4pm. Closed Dec 24–25, Jan 1. Metro: Nørreport. 10-min. walk from Christiansborg Slot up Købmagergade.

6 Buzzing **Købmagergade** and the surrounding streets offer plenty of food stalls selling hotdogs and burgers if you are after a quick snack. **Croissant'en** in Frederiksborggade does a roaring trade in tasty pizza slices.

7 ★★ **Rosenborg Slot (Rosenborg Castle).** A fairy-tale castle bang in the middle of Copenhagen, Rosenborg was built as the summer residence for Christian IV (see p 167), who moved in about 1634. The interior is opulent and largely untouched for the past 100 years, now housing the Danish Royal Collections. There are a few sights you cannot miss: fat little cherubs encrusted on the marble ceiling of room 5; Frederick IV's ornate ivory-inlaid mandolin in room

10; the strange mirrored floor of his dressing room (room 13a), and the majestic red, black, and white tiled Long Hall on the third floor. Downstairs in the Treasury, the Danish Crown Jewels sparkle in semi-darkness. The palace is surrounded with the lawns of Kongens Have (King's Gardens, see p 86), the perfect picnic venue on sunny days. ⏱ *1 hr. Øster Voldgade 4a.* ☎ *+45 3315 3286. www.rosenborgslot.dk. Admission 80DKK, 40DKK students & over 65, free under 18, free with Copenhagen Card. Tues–Sun 11am–4pm. Closed Mon; Dec 24–25, Jan 1. Metro: Nørreport. Bus 6a, 184, 185, 180S, 173E. 10-min walk from Rundetårn.*

⑧ ★★ kids Statens Museum for Kunst (National Gallery). Spanning art from the 14th century to contemporary work, this glorious light-filled gallery began life in the 19th century and nowadays has a simple glass extension linked by a wide exhibition space called Sculpture Street. Renaissance works, portraiture, and Danish art plus a few Rembrandts and Rubens are housed in the original section of the museum with modern works in the newer glass extension. Look for quality paintings by Braque, Derain, Matisse, Dufy, and Modigliano as well as the odd Picasso and interesting contemporary Danish work. A massive patchwork quilt by Kirsten Roepstorff in 1972 pre-dates Tracey Emin's similar creations by decades. ⏱ *1½ hr. Sølvgade 48-50.* ☎ *+45 3374 8494. www.smk.dk. Admission 80DKK, 60DKK over 65, 50DKK students, free under 18s, free with Copenhagen Card. Tues, Thu–Sun 10am–5pm; Wed 10am–8pm. Closed Mon; Dec 24–25, Jan 1. Metro: Nørreport. Bus 6a, 184, 185, 180S, 173E. 5-min walk from Rosenborg Slot.*

⑨ ★★ Karen Blixen Museum. Jump in the train from Østerport (5-min walk from Statens Museum) as far as Rungsted to visit the ivy-covered family home of Karen Blixen (1885–1962), Denmark's favorite lady of letters and best known to the rest of us as author of *Out of Africa*. The coach house is now converted into an exhibition of prints, photos, letters, and manuscripts charting the story of her tumultuous life; witness the striking black-and-white portrait by Cecil Beaton and

King Christian VIII's room at Rosenborg Slot.

The Karen Blixen Museum is at her country house.

cartoons featuring her with Ernest Hemingway; they shared a mutual passion for Africa. Born at Rungstedlund in 1885, Blixen moved to Kenya in 1914 with her aristocratic Swedish husband Bror von Blixen-Finecke. Controversially they divorced in 1924 and Karen returned to Denmark in 1931 after her lover Denys Finch Hatton was killed in a plane crash. Living quarters in the main house are virtually unchanged since Blixen's death in 1962. Off the hallway is a gallery hung with her paintings; the two Kikuyu portraits shine out. The rooms are pleasantly but plainly furnished, with great wood-burning stoves and Kenyan furniture. A short film showcases Blixen's life, and there are tapes of her reading her stories. The Corona typewriter she used is in the study at the front of the house. **Outside**, Blixen is buried at the bottom of Ewald's Hill in the 14-acre garden. Follow the path from the museum through the orchard and her grave is under the beech tree. ◷ *1 hr. Rungstedlund, Rungsted Strandvej 111, 2960 Rungsted Kyst.*

☎ *+45 4557 1057. www.karen-blixen. dk. Admission 45DKK, under 18s free, free with Copenhagen Card. May 1–Sept 30 Tues–Sun 10am–5pm; Oct 1–Apr 30 Wed–Fri 1pm–4pm, Sat–Sun 11am–4pm. Tours of the house half hourly. Train: Line F from Østerport to Rungsted departs every 20 minutes and the journey takes 25 minutes. It's a 20-min hike to the museum, but bus No. 388 from the station stops there. Return to Hovedbanegården (Central Station) in Copenhagen.*

🔟 **Spicylicious.** Round off a long sightseeing day in Vesterbro, just behind the station on the return from Rungsted. Order a delicious papaya salad with peanuts and chili followed by wok-fried prawns with oyster sauce and pak choi in laid-back surroundings. There's even a take-away service if you want to head straight back to your hotel. See p 101. *Istedgade 27.* ☎ *+45 3322 8533. www.restaurantspicy licious.dk. $$.* ●

Golden Age to Today

1 Den Hirschsprungske Samling
2 Statens Museum for Kunst
3 Café Republic
4 Davids Samling
5 Kunstindustrimuseet
6 Georg Jensen
7 Dansk Design Center

If you ever doubted Copenhagen's flair and commitment to the best of art and design, this tour will make you think again. You'll see some inspiring art from the Golden Age of the late 19th century, contemporary industrial design, and a whole swathe of work by iconic designers. START: **Metro or S-Tog to Nørreport and a 5-minute walk up Øster Voldgade.**

1 ★★ Den Hirschsprungske Samling. An unsung little salon and to my mind deserving more attention, specializing in Danish art from the 19th and early 20th centuries. Tobacco magnate Heinrich Hirschsprung bequeathed his collection to the nation in 1911 and it's housed in a porticoed pavilion behind the Statens Museum (see below). Ranging through a series of elegantly decorated rooms, highlights include portraits by CW Eckersberg (1783–1853), leader of a band of Golden Age painters that included Christen Købke (1810–1848) (look for his fine painting of fellow artist Frederik Sødring in Room 2). Early rooms record works by artists on the Grand Tour, later pastoral paintings depict scenes of rural bliss. For me the gallery's highlights include Kristian Zahrtman's (1843–1917) irreverent royal portraits in Room 13 and the fabulous body of work by Peder Severin Krøyer (1851–1909) in Room 21. He was the shining light of the Skagen Painters, a colony of artists who gathered in north Jutland in the late 19th century to paint the soft light there; Hirschsprung was his patron. Catch the self-portraits and the dreamy *Summer Evening at the Beach at Skagen*, which includes the artist, his wife and dog. 🕐 *1 hr. Stockholmsgade 20.* ☎ *+45 3542 0336. Admission 35DKK; 25DKK students; kids under 18 free. Free with Copenhagen Card. Wed–Mon 11am–4pm. Closed Tue. Guided tours arranged in advance. Metro: Nørreport and 5-min walk up Øster Voldgade.*

Statens Museum for Kunst.

Café Republic in Statens Museum for Kunst.

② ★★ kids **Statens Museum for Kunst.** Copenhagen's National Gallery showcases a wealth of Danish art through the ages and has a strong collection of paintings and sketches from the Golden Age (CW Eckersberg, Abildgård (1743–1809), and Hammershøi (1864–1916)) in rooms 218–229. Work by CoBrA Group artists, a pan-European group centered on Copenhagen, Brussels, and Amsterdam in the 1950s, celebrate Denmark's continuing significance in the art world. Look in Room 208 for the abstracts by Asger Jorn (1914–1973, see p 156), inspired by the darker side of Norse mythology. ⏱ *45 min. See p 21, bullet ⑧. 2-min walk across Østre Anlæg park.*

③ ★★ **Café Republic.** In the delightful modern extension to the Statens Museum, this airy, sun-filled café has views across **Østre Anlæg** gardens to a small lake. Refuel here on organic coffees and pastries, salads, and various open sandwiches. *Sølvgade 48-50.* ☎ *+45 3374 8494. $–$$.*

④ **Davids Samling.** The gallery re-opened after extensive renovation in May 2009. The extensive Islamic collection was gathered by wealthy barrister Christian Ludvig David (1878–1960), and is augmented by a splendid collection of Danish decorative arts from the 18th century onwards, covering silverware, porcelain, glassware, and portraits by Jens Juel (1745–1802) as well as Golden Age paintings by CW Eckersberg (see above). *Kronprinsessegade 30-32.* ☎ *+45 3373 4949. www.davidmus.dk. 10-min walk to the opposite side of Kongens Have.*

⑤ ★★★ kids **Kunstindustrimuseet (Danish Museum of Art and Design).** My favorite museum and best place to see the development of Danish applied arts and industrial design through the years. If you have been before, bypass the porcelain, lace, and Chinese embroidery (see p 16) to concentrate on what Danes do best; create beautiful and functional designs. There is iconic cutlery made

Taking Them Home

Serious design addicts can indulge their fancy in Copenhagen's avant-garde style shops: Hay Cph, Illums Bolighus, Normann Copenhagen, and trusty old Kartell (see p 78) all have on-trend designs for sale at sometimes reasonable prices. Art lovers can explore the galleries on **Bredgade**, but don't expect any bargains!

by Arne Jacobsen (1902–1971) for the Radisson SAS Royal Hotel (see p 132), the Platypus Dish by Henning Koppel (1918–1981), Finn Juhl (1912–1989) chairs, lots of functionalist furniture, and lighting by Verner Panton (1926–1998). Temporary exhibitions often include jewelry by young local designers. ⏲ *1 hr. See p 16, bullet ➐. Metro: Kongens Nytorv. Ten-minutes walk down Dronningens Tværgade, left on Bredgade.*

➏ ★★ **Georg Jensen.** If you've got the time on the walk down to the Rådhuspladsen, pop into Georg Jensen on Strøget (see p 82) to nose around the museum in the basement, with its roll call of silversmiths from 1904 to the present day. As well as letters and designs by Jensen (1866–1935) himself, there are exhibits by Arne Jacobsen, Henning Koppel, Søren Georg Jensen (1917–1982), and Jensen senior's main associate, Johan Rohde (1856–1935), whose designs influenced the functionalist movement of the

1930s. ⏲ *30 min. Amagertorv 4.* ☎ *+45 3311 4080. 15-minute walk across Kongens Nytorv.*

➐ ★★ **Dansk Design Center.** A light-filled, ash-floored, minimalist five-story space, part museum, part bookshop, and exhibition space created to showcase the best design talent Denmark can offer. There are 14 exhibitions annually, ranging from furniture to houseware and lighting. The permanent exhibition is tucked away in the basement; 20th-century icons include an Apple Mac from 1984, Lego, Levi jeans, and a scale-model of Concorde. Pick up a design book in the shop; it has got the most informative selection in Copenhagen. ⏲ *1 hr. HC Andersens Boulevard 27.* ☎ *+45 3369 3369. www.ddc.dk. Admission 50DKK; 25DKK students; free for kids 12–18. Free with Copenhagen Card. Mon–Tue, Thur–Fri 10am–5pm; Wed 10am–7pm; Sat–Sun 11am-4pm. Guided tours in English by pre-arrangement. 15 min from Kongens Nytorv.*

Porcelain, Danish Museum of Art and Design.

Today's Copenhagen

1. Radisson SAS Royal Hotel
2. Street Food
3. Danske Jødisk Museum
4. Den Sorte Diamant
5. Søren K
6. Det Kongelige Teater Skuespilhuset
7. Det Kongelige Teater Operaen
8. Dansk Arkitektur Center

Ever since Arne Jacobsen changed the face of Copenhagen with his radical Radisson Hotel, the city has been proud to embrace innovative architecture. New buildings have been springing up at a rate of knots, especially around the revitalized waterfront; here's a chance to tour the highlights of this thoroughly 21st-century city. START: **Bus 2A, 5A, 151 to Rådhuspladsen.**

1 ★★ **Radisson SAS Royal Hotel.** What better place to kick off a tour of Copenhagen's contemporary architecture than at the city's original boutique hotel (see p 132) and local landmark? In 1956, Arne Jacobsen, Denmark's most famous designer, had a hand in it all from the architecture (square, functional, it's not an attractive building) to the furniture and the cutlery, and so doing revolutionized Danish design concepts. At 22 stories, the Radisson was briefly Scandinavia's tallest building, and the windows stretch around the rooms like ribbons, giving views over Copenhagen's rooftops. Jacobsen moved into room 606 for a while, before taking a violent dislike to his handiwork and moving out. Following renovations, few elements of his original designs remain, but room 606 has been preserved (ask at reception if you want to have a look at it). Nevertheless, his Swan, Pot and Egg chairs, cutlery, and

crockery are regarded as timeless classics; they have been copied by many hotels and are sold in many Copenhagen shops (see p 71).
🕐 *40 min. 5-min walk from Rådhuspladsen. See p 132 for details.*

2 **Street Food.** Stave off mid-morning hunger pangs with a sizzling hot dog from one of Strøget's countless street stalls and eat it in the gardens of the Kongelige Bibliotek, which is in front of the Jewish Museum.

3 ★★ **Danske Jødisk Museum (Danish Jewish Museum).** Designed by American architect Daniel Libeskind (b. 1946), who has drawn up plans for Ground Zero in New York, this museum occupies the Royal Boat House of Christian IV, who invited the Sephardic Jews to Denmark from Portugal in 1622. The

The Black Diamond leans over the Øresund.

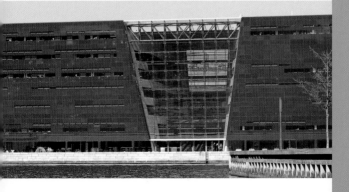

The Royal Danish Playhouse.

boathouse was subsequently enveloped in the Kongelige Bibliotek (Royal Library) when it was built in 1906. Opened in 2004, the Jewish Museum's interior is as innovative as the exterior is traditional. The interconnecting wooden passageways tip at crazy angles, conflicting with the display cases, which point in all directions. The pod-like interconnections museum sections represent the close relationship between the Danes and the Jews after they were helped to flee Denmark in WW2. ⏱ *30 min. 20-min walk from Rådhuspladsen up Strøget; look at the diverse architecture as you go. See p 19, bullet* ❹.

❹ ★★★ **Den Sorte Diamant (Black Diamond).** Housed in the same complex as the Jewish Museum, the Black Diamond houses part of the Royal Library. The Library has 4.5 million books accessible to the public and is the largest in Scandinavia, with rare manuscripts by national treasures Karen Blixen, Hans Christian Andersen, and Søren Kierkegaard. I think it's one of Copenhagen's most spectacular sights, best seen by boat as you emerge from Christianshavn Kanal (see p 63). The building bends over the sparkling Øresund, with a glass and granite-clad frontage reflecting the waves and boats as they pass by. Built by

architects Schmidt, Hammer and Lassen and opened in 1999, there's also a bookshop, concerts in the Queen's Hall, exhibition space, and a highly rated restaurant **Søren K** (see below). ⏱ *1 hr. Søren Kierkegårds Plads 1.* ☎ *+45 3347 4747. www.kb. dk. Admission to library free. Exhibitions 40DKK; 25DKK students; free for kids under 16. Exhibitions: Mon–Fri 10am–7pm; Sat 10am–5pm. Library: Jan 3–June 30 & Sept 1–Dec 22 9am–9pm; Sat 9am–5pm. Jul 1–Aug 15 9am–7pm. 5 minutes walk from Jewish Museum.*

❺ **Søren K.** Expensive (see p 101) but worth it for the views over the Øresund from the first floor of the Black Diamond (see above) and the minimalist gray décor. It's international cuisine of the highest level. Enjoy a late lunch or book for dinner. *Søren Kierkegaards Plads 1.* ☎ *+45 3347 4949. $$$.*

❻ ★★★ **Det Kongelige Teater Skuespilhuset (Royal Danish Playhouse).** A triumphant success for Danish architects Lundgård and Tranberg, this theater opened in 2008. Personally the Playhouse (see p 122) reminds me of a squat glass box with a wooden-clad brick sitting on top of it; albeit a box with

Other Places to See

Copenhagen's newest quarter of Ørestaden is rising phoenix-like from an industrial wasteland between the motorway and railway. With a concept initially conceived by Daniel Libeskind (see p 169), highlights include two curved 20-story high-rises surrounding a central square, apartments, offices, restaurants, bars, and shops; it's Copenhagen's answer to the Western Harbor development in Malmö (see p 150). One Metro stop away on the island of Amager, Jean Nouvel's revolutionary **DR City** concert hall (see p 117) is taking shape. Take bus route no 388 from Rådhuspladsen to Vilvordevej to see the Zaha Hadid-designed new gallery at **Ordrupgaard Museum of French Impressionism,** reminiscent of Future Systems' Natwest Media Centre at Lords Cricket Ground in London.

splendid vistas of the Øresund and Operaen across the water. Despite its appearance, the people of Copenhagen have taken their new theater to their hearts and its pier is a great place to stroll; the wooden waterfront is to be extended along the Øresund by 2010. ⏱ *45 min. See p 122. 10-min wander along the waterfront.*

⑦ ★★★ Det Kongelige Teater Operaen (Opera House). With first performances in 2005 on a

The glass frontage of the Operaen.

man-made island at Dokøen directly opposite Amalienborg (see p 15), the Opera House (see p 119) was not an immediate success with the Danish public, but as the infrastructure has improved around it, the building has become more popular. Its cantilevered roof and semi-circular frontage, designed by Henning Larson, looks spectacular when lit up at night. To explore inside, book a guided tour in advance (☎ +45 3369 6933, www.operaen.dk). They run Sat–Sun 9.30am and 4.30pm and cost 100DKK to see the spacious interior. ⏱ *45 min. See p 119. Movia harbor boat service from Nyhavn to Holmen.*

⑧ ★ Dansk Arkitektur Center. Still on the island of Holmen but further south in Christianshavn, this venue provides an overview of Danish architecture through a series of temporary exhibitions and publications; the center is publicly funded and calls itself a 'visionarium'. Have a browse around Denmark's potential new landmarks. ⏱ *45 min. Strandgade 27B. ☎ +45 3257 1930. www.dac.dk. Free admission. Daily 10am–5pm; Wed 10am–9pm. 15-min walk from Operaen.*

Copenhagen & Kids

1 Tivoli
2 Tivoli food stalls
3 The Wonderful World of Hans Christian Andersen
4 Nationalmuseet
5 Street Theater
6 Guinness World Records Museum
7 Post & Tele Museum
8 Café Hovedtelegrafen
9 Tøjhusmuseet
10 Zoo
11 Grill at Café K
12 IMAX Tycho Brahe Planetarium

I find Copenhagen an easy place to get around: traffic is light, the center is pedestrianized, and the pace is fairly laid-back for a capital city: that's why I recommend it for families. There are lots of museums to appeal to kids, plenty to do outdoors and of course there's Tivoli, with its amusement arcades and roller coaster rides. If the list below seems excessive for families, pick and choose according to the age and interests of your kids. START: **Bus 2A, 5A, 151 to Rådhuspladsen.**

1 ★★★ kids Tivoli. Where all children will want to start, Tivoli is as enticing by day as it is by night (see p 88). Get there for 11am to see the Tivoli Boys Guard Parade (Wed, Sat, Sun) playing 'ompah' music. There are several points in the park to buy multi-ride tickets (see p 10 for prices), which allow you to try the rides as often as you want. If, like me, shooting through the pitch black on the Roller-Coaster is quite extreme enough, take toddlers for a gentle underwater adventure with Nemo on the Nautilus carousel or for a potter on the Dragon Boats. A slow underground trundle past dragons and mice in The Mine is perfect for little ones but most teenagers determinedly head straight for The Star Flyer, which rises to spin 80m above Copenhagen; try it if you dare; if you can keep your eyes open the views of Copenhagen are spectacular! ⏱ 2 hrs. See p 10, bullet 8.

2 Tivoli food stalls. With all the choice Tivoli offers, a mid-morning ice cream or candy-floss from any stall around the fairground rides will go down extremely well.

3 ★ kids The Wonderful World of Hans Christian Andersen. An experience aimed directly at kids. Born in Odense in 1805, Andersen arrived in Copenhagen in 1819 determined to be an actor (see p 44). He didn't get his

Tivoli Boys Guard by the garden entrance.

The Wonderful World of Hans Christian Andersen.

big theatrical break but in 1835 wrote his first whimsical fairy tale, *The Tinder Box*. In this museum you'll find scenes from his early life and tableaux of his stories *Thumbelina* and *The Tin Soldier* for children to enjoy alongside the original manuscript for *The Stone of the Wise*

Postman from 1956 collecting letters on his motorbike at the Post & Tele Museum.

Man, the museum's most costly purchase and found in the Legacy Room. This attraction is in the same building as Ripley's Believe it or Not!—I thought it was ghastly. Two-headed cow? No thanks. Avoid at all costs unless the kids insist. 🕐 *45 min. See p 13, bullet ❶. 5-min walk from Tivoli.*

❹ ★ **Nationalmuseet.** Denmark's National Museum is Scandinavia's largest, set within a vast, rambling one-time palace. Here younger kids can attend a 1940s' Danish school in the first-floor Children's Museum (rooms 51–55) and try on clothes worn when their grandparents were young. Boys clamber over the full-size model of a Viking ship, while budding fashion queens can dress up as princesses in pink tutus. There's a well-labeled prehistoric collection, housing a fabled Iron Age Sun Chariot, a Bronze Age girl's grave and musical instruments. Entry to the museum is free so there's no need to feel you have to see everything at once—children may rebel! 🕐 *2 hrs. See p 9, bullet ❼. 5-min walk down Rådhuspladsen.*

❺ ★★★ kids **Street Theater.** Most days see some sort of entertainment along Copenhagen's pedestrian zed main drag, be it mime artists, jugglers, or musicians. Even watching the rickshaw peddlers and cyclists steer around the crowds on Hojbrø Plads is amusing. 🕙 15 min.

6 kids **Guinness World Records Museum.** You may love it or hate it but the sight of the world's tallest man standing outside the museum makes it irresistible to kids. The well-trodden formula here (man with longest moustache, most prolific sow) is at least enlivened by a sports gallery, in which various games test physical strength; there's a truly awful waxwork of the Danish Royal Family that made me giggle too. 🕙 45 min. Østergade 16. ☎ +45 3332 3131. www.top attractions.dk. Admission 85DKK, 68DKK kids 11–14, 43DKK kids 4–10. Free with Copenhagen Card. Jan 2–June 14 & Sept 1–Dec 31 Sun–Thurs 10am–6pm, Fri–Sat 10am–8pm; June 15–Aug 31 daily 10am–8pm. 15-min walk along Strøget.

7 ★★ kids **Post & Tele Museum.** Telling the story of Danish communications systems from 1587 to present—mail coach to mobile—this museum absorbs the attention of young boys with tableaux, old photos, lots of smart uniforms, and motorbikes. Highlights for me were the pumpkin-shaped horse-drawn mail coach, a replica iceboat used for transporting letters through wintry waters, and a proud postman from the 1950s, complete with strange headgear and bright-yellow bike. Temporary exhibitions offer lots of interactive fun for kids into time machines, flashing lights and beeping noises. 🕙 1 hr. Købmagergade 37. ☎ +45 3341 0900. www.ptt-museum. dk. Admission 50DKK; 40DKK seniors; 25DKK students; free for kids under 18. Free with Copenhagen Card. Tue, Thur–Sat 10am–5pm; Wed 10am–8pm; Sun 12pm–4pm. 5-min walk from Østergade.

8 ★★★ kids **Café Hovedtele-grafen.** This fifth-floor museum café is a cut above the average. I ordered tiger prawns, smoked salmon, and tuna wasabi—it was excellent and very fresh, but there are lots of simple dishes catering to young appetites, such as burgers and chicken rolls. Grab a seat on the terrace for views towards the Rundetårn (see p 20). Købmagergade 37. ☎ +45 3341 0900. www.cafehoved telegrafen.dk. $$.

9 ★ kids **Tøjhusmuseet (Royal Danish Arsenal Museum).** Part of the **Slotsholmen museum complex** (see p 19), this is another winner for boys who hold a fascination for military paraphernalia. Stored in the vaulted palace arsenal opened by Christian IV in 1604, canons, machine guns and mortars line the walls. Upstairs in the Armory Hall,

The wooden observation tower at the zoo.

Outdoor Kids

Many other Copenhagen museums and galleries have children's workshops, including **Louisiana** (see p 154), **Statens Museum for Kunst** (see p 21), and the **Danish Kunstindustrimuseet**, where there are lots of opportunities for getting good and dirty while learning. There are loads of open green spaces where kids can let off steam; **Kongens Have** (see p 86) and **Frederiksberg Have** (see p 87) have play areas for toddlers, and the **Lakes** (see p 86) are good for afternoon strolls. **Canal tours** (see p 7) always go down a treat, as will the artificial beach at Havnebadet (see p 85), the soft sands of **Amager Beach**, and the grazing deer at **Dyrehaven** (see p 87). Older children are perfectly safe getting around the city-center cycle lanes by **bike**; younger ones will enjoy **rickshaw rides**—pick one up at the north end of Nyhavn on Kongens Nytorv. There is an ageing amusement park (it's actually Europe's oldest) at **Bakken** *(Dyrehavevej 62, 2930 Klampenborg,* ☎ *+ 45 3963 3544)* 12km north of Copenhagen, with lots of thrills and spills, but frankly this has seen better days. I would choose Tivoli every time.

there are uniforms, ceremonial swords and guns, plus a distinctly unpleasant but oddly fascinating exhibition about famous assassinations. This is due to be replaced (I hope with something less macabre) by 2012. 🕐 *1 hr. Tøjhus 3.* ☎ *+45 3311 6037. www.thm.dk. Admission 50DKK, 40DKK seniors, 25DKK students, free for kids under 18. Free with Copenhagen Card. Tue, Thur–Sat 10am–5pm; Wed 10am–8pm; Sun 12pm–4pm. 5-min walk from Østergade.*

🔟 ★★ **kids** Zoo. Although the greatest attraction at the Zoo right now is the Norman Foster elephant house, that's just the beginning for youngsters. With 3,000 animals, the zoo is divided into zones (Africa, Birds, etc.) so kids can understand where animals come from and the conditions they inhabit naturally. Climb the observation tower to get your bearings and you'll be rewarded with fine views over

Frederiksberg Have and beyond to the city center. The Children's Zoo has pygmy goats and a small pony track for toddler rides, plus an enclosure for cuddling rabbits. There are shows on the Zoo Stage every day during school holidays. Feeding times are also popular attractions: chimps at 3.30pm (not Friday), seals at 10am and 2.30pm (2pm on Friday). I also saw birds of prey flying to catch their feed at 1pm. Check at the entrance gate for times. 🕐 *2 hrs. 10-min walk to Rådhuspladsen and bus 6A or 26. See p 88, bullet* ⓫.

⓫ **Grill at Café K.** There's a simple brunch menu for kids at the café: pancake, yogurt, cheese, and fruit. Barbecues can be cooked on the grill outside on the terrace in summer. *To pre-order a BBQ, call* ☎ *+45 3646 6060.*

The IMAX dome at Tycho Brahe Planetarium.

⓬ ★★★ kids IMAX Tycho Brahe Planetarium. Round off a long day relaxing under the stars (literally) in the Planetarium's Space Theatre. With 10 shows a day up until 9pm, the IMAX shows begin with a presentation of the night sky—perfect for budding astronomers. There's a small science exhibition on the ground floor, as well as a changing choice of superb short 3-D films in the cinema off the foyer (see p 118). I sat through the fantastic *Cosmic Coaster*, twice as it took the audience on a high-velocity dash across the galaxy. 🕑 *1 hr. Bus 6A or 26 back to Rådhuspladsen and 5-min walk. See p 118.*

Out of Town Treats

The Experimentarium is an interactive museum that somehow makes science attractive to children—and that can't be bad. Lots of hands-on exhibits and knowledgeable staff (called 'pilots') are there to answer your questions. *Tuborg Havnevej 7, 2900 Hellerup.* ☎ *+45 3927 3333. www.experimentarium.dk. Bus 388.* **Danmarks Akvarium** has a series of themed aquariums and a touching pool of rays for children to stroke. Opens weekends and during school holidays. *Kavalérgåden 1, 2920 Charlottelund.* ☎ *+45 3962 3283. www. akvarium.dk.* The new eco-friendly **Blue Planet Aquarium** with a 'whirlwind' design by Danish architects 3XN will open in 2013 on the coast at Kastrup Havn.

Royal Copenhagen

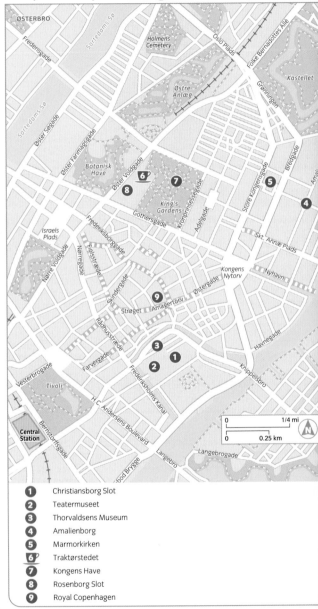

❶	Christiansborg Slot
❷	Teatermuseet
❸	Thorvaldsens Museum
❹	Amalienborg
❺	Marmorkirken
❻	Traktørstedet
❼	Kongens Have
❽	Rosenborg Slot
❾	Royal Copenhagen

Never a family to settle down anywhere for long, the Danish Royals built castles in the way that some women collect handbags. The extraordinary legacy left by generations of kings eager to make their mark is felt all over Copenhagen, in their splendid palaces, polished museums, and priceless collections of heirlooms. START: **Metro to Kongens Nytorv.**

❶ ★★ **Christiansborg Slot.** On the island of **Slotsholmen, where Bishop Absalon** (see p 167) founded Copenhagen in 1160–1167 and built his first stronghold, Christiansborg Palace serves as the ceremonial headquarters of the Danish Royal Family as well as being the seat the Folketinget, Danish parliament. There were four previous buildings on the site. Absalon's Palace went up in smoke in 1367; visit the remains under the present palace (see p 19). Its replacement, fortified Copenhagen Castle, was demolished by King Christian VI (see p 167) in 1731 to make way for his flamboyant baroque statement palace; sadly that did not see the century out before burning down in 1794. A second, even more splendid palace was destroyed by fire in 1884, although the chapel survived unscathed until 1992 before itself succumbing to fire. Today's palace dates from 1928 and at one time had the tallest tower in the city, at 106m. The grand **Royal Reception Rooms** on the second floor are scene of gala dinners, presidential visits and ambassadorial meetings. Tapestries and murals adorn some walls, others are covered in historical oil paintings, marble busts and fine furniture fill every

room. ⏱ *50 min. Prins Jørgens Gård 1* ☎ *+45 3392 6492. www.ses. dk. Admission: 65DKK, 55DKK students; 30DKK kids 7–14. May 1–Sept 30 daily 10am–4pm. Oct 1–Apr 30 Tue–Sun 10am–4pm. 10-min walk from Kongens Nytorv.*

❷ ★ **Teatermuseet (Theater Museum).** After the original Christiansborg Palace was finished by German architect Elias David Häusser (1687–1745) in 1745, the space above the Royal Stables was converted into a theater for the Court, which opened in 1767. It was refurbished 1842, and still contains plush red stalls and leather seats. There's not a huge amount to see; programs and posters, a few costumes, and an old wind machine that still works, but you can wander the auditorium and go backstage to watch some black-and-white film

King Christian IX's statue at Christiansborg Slot.

Family & Friends

The Danes are sweetly sentimental about their Royal Family and don't appreciate criticism of the Queen. On her birthday (April 16), I joined the crowds gathering in their thousands under the balcony of her palace to cheer her and sing happy birthday as she waved grandly from above. Whenever Queen Margrethe is in residence at Amalienborg, soldiers stationed at Rosenborg Slot (see p 20) march regally between the two castles to change the guards at midday.

footage. ⏱ *30 min. Christiansborg Ridebane 18.* ☎ *+45 3311 5176. Admission 30DKK, 20DKK seniors and students, free under 18. Free with Copenhagen Card. Tue, Thur 11am–3pm; Wed 11am–7pm; Sat–Sun 1pm–4pm. In the courtyard of the palace.*

❸ ★ Thorvaldsens Museum. Bertel Thorvaldsen (c.1770–1844) was born in Denmark but spent much of his working life as a much-praised neoclassical sculptor in Rome. In 1837 he returned to Copenhagen a wealthy man and

bequeathed his art collection and many of his own sculpture to the city. The collection is housed in an elegant neoclassic-influenced building designed by Gottlieb Bindesbøll and opened in 1848 on the site of the old Royal Coach House. The side facing Gammel Strand is decorated with scenes of Thorvaldsen's triumphant return to Copenhagen; spot his contemporary Hans Christian Andersen raising his hat in the crowds! The three-story museum is arranged around a courtyard containing Thorvaldsen's grave and

Thorvaldsens Museum.

The Queen's Palace, Amalienborg.

exhibits hundreds of busts, marble statues, and relief work, all neoclassical in style, along with an assortment of religious and romantic paintings. Although the collection is phenomenal, to my mind the most special element of the museum is the intricate plasterwork and decoration covering the interior. On the second floor, stand at the end of one of the long galleries to admire the blue ceiling and plaster work, the ornate marble floors, and the sun flooding in on to the sculptures lining the walls. 🕘 *1 hr. Bertel Thorvaldsens Plads 2.* 📞 *+ 45 3332 1532. www.thorvaldsensmuseum.dk. Admission: 40DKK, 10DKK seniors. Free Wed and with Copenhagen Card. Tue–Sun 10am–5pm. 5-min walk from Christiansborg.*

❹ ★★ **Amalienborg.** Take a stroll through Kongens Nytorv—the King's Square—and down Bredgade to Amalienborg, the complex of four virtually identical palaces bordering a massive octagonal cobbled square—the winter residence of the Royal Family. They took a fancy to the palaces in 1794 after Christiansborg burned down again (see p 39), which was unfortunate for the aristocratic families who had them built by Nicolas Eigtved (see p 15) in the

1750s. To the left as you enter the square, Christian VIII's palace is partly open to the public (see p 15). To its left, the interior of Brockdorff's Palace was designed by Bertel Thorvaldsen (see p 40) in his early career. The statue of Frederik V posing as a Roman emperor was the work of French sculptor JJ Saly. It was unveiled to the public in 1771 by Frederik's son, Christian VII, who later halted construction work on

Entrance to the Marmorkirken on Bredgade.

The red brick Rosenborg Castle.

and fine altar or at the weekend join the climb to the top of the dome. It's worth the struggle up 150 steps for the views over the palace complex, the golden onion domes of the Russian Orthodox church next door and Rosenborg Slot in the distance. Not suitable for those afraid of heights. ⏲ *30 min. Tours Sat–Sun 1pm and 3pm. See p 16, bullet* ⑥. *Across Bredgade from Amalienborg.*

⑥ ★★ **Traktørstedet.** Grab a table on the pretty terrace for regal views of Rosenborg Castle over coffee and freshly baked cakes or a glass of wine. There's also an excellent lunch menu with a range of *smørrebrød*, salads, and steaks. It's the only restaurant I know where the candles come in little coronets. *Øster Volgade 4a.* ☎ *+45 3315 7620. $–$$.*

the Marmorkirken (see below and p 16) when the coffers ran dry on Frederik's master plan to aggrandize the palace complex. Royal Guards parade in two-hour shifts outside all four palaces. ⏲ *30 min. See p 15, bullet* ⑤. *20-min walk through the city center.*

⑤ ★ **Marmorkirken (Marble Church).** A step away from Amalienborg, this circular church's massive copper dome (see p 16) is a local landmark. When in residence, the Queen attends services here. Drop by to look at the painted ceiling

⑦ ★★ **kids Kongens Have.** If you would prefer to picnic on a sunny day, here's the perfect spot. The formal gardens were commissioned by Christian IV in the 17th century to surround his summer palace (see below). Otto Heider drew up the originals plans but fashions in landscaping changed over the years; a lane of trees has been planted leading to the castle and

Royal Connections

The royals certainly liked their creature comforts; other homes include **Kronborg Palace** in Helsingør (see p 146), **Fredensborg**, the Queen's summer home (the gardens are open to the public in July, see www.ses.dk for details), and romantic **Frederiksborg Palace** at Hillerød (see p 142). **Roskilde Cathedral** is the traditional burial place of kings and queens (see p 141) and, back in Copenhagen, the 18th-century summer palace at **Frederiksberg** (see p 53) has landscaped gardens that make an ideal spot for a stroll in the summer sun.

Flora Danica.

the formal parterres in front of the castle now serve as parade ground for the soldiers living in barracks next door. There is an adventure playground for kids and a puppet theater on the edge of the gardens (see p 117). 🕐 *45 min. See p 86, bullet* ❺*. 5-min walk along Dronningens Tværgade.*

Royal Copenhagen.

❽ ★★ **Rosenborg Slot**. Partly built by Hans van Steenwinckel, Christian IV's architect, the Rosenborg Castle continued to grow over many years. With the engaging Royal Danish Collection, the interior of this ornate red-brick castle brims with royal paintings, fine furniture, and tapestries in rooms decorated in Renaissance and rococo styles. Royal Copenhagen fans can head to room 23 to see rare Flora Danica porcelain (see p 145). In the Treasury, you'll be impressed by Christian IV's ostentatious saddle and the Crown Jewels, encrusted with vast diamonds, sapphires, and garnets. 🕐 *1½ hr. See p 20, bullet* ❼*.

❾ ★ **Royal Copenhagen**. If you fancy taking home a piece of modern Flora Danica china (the original flower-patterned service was commissioned in 1790, see p 145), pop into the Royal Copenhagen store on Strøget. Upstairs there is a fine collection but you might be taken aback by the price! It is possibly the world's most expensive china. Best to make do with some of Royal Copenhagen's timeless blue-and-white pattern. 🕐 *130 min. See p 76. 20-min walk.*

Hans Christian Andersen

① Hans Christian Andersen Statue
② Tivoli
③ The Wonderful World of Hans Christian Andersen
④ Café à Porta
⑤ Thorvaldsens Museum
⑥ Magasin du Nord
⑦ Det Kongelige Teater
⑧ Hotel D'Angleterre
⑨ Nyhavn
⑩ Little Mermaid
⑪ Restaurant Els

Denmark's favorite literary son was born in Odense in 1805 but lived in Copenhagen for many years in between European jaunts and sojourns with aristocratic Danish friends. He arrived in the city in 1819 to seek his fortune as an actor; when that career stalled he turned to writing, scoring a hit in 1829 with *A Journey on Foot from Holmen's Canal to the East Point of Amager*, before meeting with wild success with *Fairy Tales* in 1835. Oddly enough, he never bought a property, despite the immense wealth brought to him from his fairy tales, but moved around a series of apartments in town. His influence is everywhere; in statues, his own museum, in Tivoli, and on the blue plaques that mark his many homes. START: **Rådhuspladsen.**

1 ★★ **Hans Christian Andersen Statue.** Sandwiched between the Rådhus (see p 13) and Tivoli, Andersen sits ruminatively gazing over towards Tivoli attired in top hat and formal clothes, on the boulevard that bears his name. ⏲ *5 min.*

2 ★★★ **kids Tivoli.** Tivoli has a ride dedicated to Andersen's memory. The Flying Trunk presents 32 scenes from his stories; kids can have fun guessing what they are. ⏲ *20 min. See p 10, bullet* **8**. *Across the road from the HCA statue.*

3 ★ **kids The Wonderful World of Hans Christian Andersen.** A must for all young and self-respecting Andersen fans for the simple way his life is portrayed in tableaux. Despite the apparent gentleness of his fairytales, Andersen was reputedly a bit of a curmudgeon, which can be glimpsed in his portraits; he wears a haughty demeanor. ⏲ *45 min. See p 13, bullet* **1**. *5-min walk from Tivoli.*

4 ★★★ **Café à Porta.** Andersen lived three floors above the bar between 1866–1869, when it was known as Mini's and would often pop in for a takeaway on his way home from the Royal Theatre (see below). See p 94. *Kongens Nytorv 17.* ☎ *+45 3311 0305. www.cafe aporta.dk. $$$.*

Andersen glancing over to Tivoli.

5 ★ **Thorvaldsens Museum.** Andersen and Bertel Thorvaldsen (ca 1770—1844) were leading lights in the Danish Golden Age. The storyteller is depicted in the frieze on the museum's outside wall, raising his hat in greeting to his old friend. ⏲ *10 min. See p 40, bullet* **3**. *15-min walk.*

6 ★ **Magasin du Nord.** Now a middle-of-the-road department store (see p 77), Du Nord was a hotel in Andersen's day. He lived there in the attic, writing his salutary tales

Andersen's Grave

Andersen died of cancer and his funeral at Vor Frue Kirke (Copenhagen Cathedral, see p 61) on August 11 1875 was attended by thousands after King Christian IX declared a day of national mourning. His final resting place is at plot 31 in **Assistens Kierkegård**, marked by a simple tombstone. *Kapelvej 4, Nørrebro. Bus 5A or 350S from Rådhuspladsen.*

and gaining recognition, from 1838 to 1847. 🕐 *30 min. See p 77. 5-min walk.*

❼ ★★★ Det Kongelige Teater. Despite never realizing his adolescent dreams to be an actor, Andersen had 28 plays performed here and *The Little Mermaid* was performed as a ballet. The Royal Theatre was the center of his world and during his time in the Hotel du Nord his rooms overlooked it. A marble bust in the foyer of the theater marks his influence. 🕐 *10 min. See p 122. Opposite Magasin du Nord.*

❽ ★★★ Hotel D'Angleterre. Andersen stayed several times in this opulent hotel (see p 130); during 1860 in ground-floor rooms on the corner of Østergade. From here he could see his beloved Royal Theatre across Kongens Nytorv. He returned in 1869 and 1871, using the hotel as a stop-gap before moving in with aristocratic friends. 🕐 *10 min. See p 130. Opposite Royal Theatre.*

❾ ★★★ kids Nyhavn 18, 20 & 67. Several houses along Nyhavn saw Andersen as a lodger. In 1834 he moved to number 20, settling for four years before moving to Hotel du Nord. 1848 saw him back at Nyhavn at 67, where he remained for 17 years. Later in life he spent another two years at number 20, leaving in 1873. Numbers 20 and 67 have commemorative plaques. 🕐 *20 min. See p 7. Off Kongens Nytorv.*

❿ ★★★ kids Little Mermaid. Copenhagen's number-one tourist site was unveiled in 1913. Paid for by brewing heir Carl Jacobsen and sculpted by Edvard Eriksen, the statue pays homage to Andersen's sad tale *The Little Mermaid*, published in 1836. 🕐 *10 min. See p 59, bullet ⓬. 30-min walk along Langelinie.*

⓫ Restaurant Els. In Andersen's time Els (see p 99) was known as Grandjean's Patisserie and he was so fond of the place that he wrote a poem about it. Little has changed inside since then, including the frescoes of dancing ladies on the walls. *Store Strandstræde 3.* ☎ *+45 3314 1341. www.restaurant-els.dk. $$$.* ●

Restaurant Els.

Vesterbro to Frederiksberg

1. Københavns Bymuseum
2. Bang & Jensen
3. Elephant Tower
4. Carlsberg Visitors Centre & The Jacobsen Brewhouse
5. Søndermarken
6. Picnic
7. Cisternerne—Museet for Moderne Glaskunst
8. Zoo
9. Frederiksberg Slot
10. Frederiksberg Have
11. Storm P Museet

Regeneration of the once Bohemian area around the gritty Vesterbro is happening at a phenomenal pace, with bars and cafés, ethnic shops and restaurants opening almost daily. Around the Carlsberg Brewery, one of the oldest in the world, the atmosphere changes as you enter smart Frederiksberg, with its royal connections and expansive mansion-lined boulevards. START: **Bus 6A or 26 to Vesterbro Torv.**

❶ ★★ kids Københavns Bymuseum (Museum of Copenhagen). A colorful and chaotic romp through Copenhagen's history, with five permanent exhibitions peeling back the layers of time until we arrive, in the 11th century, at the birth of the city. To me the best part of the museum deals with the thriving middle classes from 1660 to 1849; an early flair for the decorative arts is already evident in the silverware, guild cups, and the fine burgomasters' furniture on display. Upstairs there is a handful of the possessions (and some snide caricatures) of existentialist author and self-proclaimed genius Søren Kierkegård, who lived in Copenhagen for most of his life. Born in 1813, he collapsed on a city street and subsequently died in 1855 at the tender age of 42, but not before he had given the world his famous novel

Either/Or. Outside the grand museum building, dating from 1787 and originally home of the Royal Shooting Society, there is a model of the city as it appeared in medieval times, surrounded by its ring of defensive canals. ⏱ *1 hr. Vesterbrogade 59.* ☎ *+45 3321 0772. Admission 20DKK, 10DKK seniors, free for children under 17. Free with Copenhagen Card. Free Fri. Mon, Thur–Sun 10am–4pm. Wed 10am–9pm.*

❷ ★ kids Bang & Jensen. Round the corner and down Oehlenschlægersgade onto Istegade, it's time for a reviving coffee and continental buffet breakfast (served before 10.30am) in mellow surroundings (see p 93). *Istedgade 130* ☎ *+45 3325 5318. www.bangogjensen.dk. $.*

Bang & Jensen.

Model of medieval Copenhagen at Københavns Bymuseum.

③ ★★★ kids Elephant Tower.
Walk past lots of ethnic shops and cafés down Istegade towards the Carlsberg brewery complex. Soon you'll trek up a long hill towards the Elephant Tower at the New Carlsberg Brewery, which was founded in 1889 by Carl Jacobsen. This tower is attractively set off by four life-size Bernini-esque granite elephants, one at each corner. Built in 1901 by Vilhelm Dahlerup, the elephants are

Elephant tower at Carlsberg Brewery.

a metaphor for Carl Jacobsen's loyalty and philanthropy towards his workers and his country. *5-min photo opportunity. Ny Carlsberg Vej.*

④ ★★★ kids Carlsberg Visitors Centre & The Jacobsen Brewhouse. Established in 1847 by Jacob Jacobsen and named after his son Carl; for years the family has been a powerful force for good within Copenhagen, building housing for their workers and donating the fabulous Ny Carlsberg Glyptotek to the city (see p 14). The complex consists of two breweries, offices, laboratories, an academy, plus a small museum relating Carlsberg family history; the latter doesn't have much general appeal. Instead head to the Visitor Centre, established in the Old Brewery, which was built in 1847. The center provides a thoroughly up-to-date and enjoyable, interactive journey through the history of brewing at Carlsberg. Proceedings kick off with a display of 13,000 bottles of limited edition beers and rattle past steam engines, the cooperage (where the beer barrels were made), bottling displays, and a short film on cleaning the huge wooden barrels used to store the beer. In the stables, lots of

What's That All About?

On the corner of Oehlenschlægersgade (try pronouncing that!) and Kaalundsgade, look out for the bar called Art and Color, completely covered inside and out with riotous mosaics by the late Nigerian artist Mustapha Manuel Tafat. This mad mosaic-maker's work is somehow reminiscent of Gaudí's flamboyant decorative tiling in Barcelona's Parc Güell and is presently the subject of a preservation order.

contented chestnut Jutland heavy horses munch on their hay; they are still used to pull brewery drays around the city and get to travel the world promoting the brewery. The tour ends up at the Jacobsen Brewhouse (see p 107), a vast pine-floored barn with a gleaming tear-shaped copper bar, where there is a choice of lagers on sale. We got there quite late in the afternoon and it was obvious that several parties had been there for some time! ⏱ *1½ hr Gamle Carlsberg Vej 11.* ☎ *+45 3327 1282. www.visitcarlsberg.dk. Admission 50DKK, 35DKK youths 12-18, free for children under 12. Ticket includes two vouchers for beer. Tue–Sun*

Atmospheric lighting at the Cisternene.

10am–4pm. 20-min walk along Iste-gade and Ny Carlsberg Vej or S-Tog to straight to Enghave from Hoved-banegården (Central Station).

⑤ ★★ kids Søndermarken.
Pretty Søndermarken is a wild area of untamed greenery forming part of western Copenhagen's green lungs, and flanking Frederiks Have at the castle (see below). Its grassy slopes are criss-crossed with paths, with part of the zoo taking up the far end of the gardens. Walk around the edge of the zoo to get free views of ostriches and antelopes. *10-min walk up Ny Carlsberg Vej.*

Frederiksberg Slot from Sondermarken.

6 ★★★ **Picnic.** Choose a luscious organic picnic from the local branch of **Emmery's** (see p 80) at *Vesterbrogade 34* and munch by the fountain in Søndermarken. $.

7 ★★★ **Cisternerne–Museet for Moderne Glaskunst (Museum of Modern Glass Art).** Housed underneath a glass pyramid in the middle of the Søndermarken lawns, this museum of modern glassware was once the underground cistern providing water to Frederiksberg Slot across the road. The exhibits are softly illuminated from behind, sending waves of color through the sepulchral gloom. The spectacular glass creations of Faeroese artist Tróndur Patursson are memorable for their colors and vibrancy. A word of warning: water drips constantly over the floor; don't wear flip flops! ⏰ 45 min. Søndermarken. ☎ +45 3321 9310. www.cisternerne.dk. Admission 50DKK, 40DKK seniors & students, free for children under 14. Thur–Fri 2pm–6pm; Sat–Sun 11am–5pm. Underneath Søndermarkern.

8 ★★ **kids Zoo.** If you haven't already visited the zoo, drop by to see the Norman Foster elephant house. It's worth noting that the zoo occupies both sides of Roskildevej and is one of the oldest and largest in Europe, with over 2,500 animals. Its reputation as a breeding center for rare species is second to none although sadly not all animals have yet got as much room to roam as the elephants. *See p 88, bullet* **11**. *Free with Copenhagen Card. Across Roskildevej from Søndermarken.*

9 **Frederiksberg Slot.** Largely built by 1669 under the eye of King Frederik IV, and much expanded until it reached its present extent in 1735 during the reign of Christian VI, this splendid ocher-colored palace was utilized as the Royal Family's summer residence, until the 1852, when it was taken over as a military academy. It occupies a dramatic position over-looking the sloping landscaped lawns of Frederiksberg Have and in the distance you can see the rides of Tivoli. Getting inside the castle requires planning; opening hours are limited to the last Saturday of the month (11am–1pm by guided tour only) but it's worth the effort to see the ornate Baroque interior of the palace chapel, hidden in the east wing. *Roskildevej 28.* ☎ *+45 3616 2244. Next to the zoo.*

⑩ ★★★ kids Frederiksberg Have. From the castle, head off through the bucolic delights of Frederiksberg's manicured French classical style gardens with English landscaping (see p 87). Once the playground of royalty, they now brim over with family life at the weekends; in summer take a lake tour by rowing boat from the front of the castle. Turn left towards the back of the zoo to the Temple of Apis, a mock-Palladian folly built in 1806—from here you can glimpse the Chinese Pavilion among the trees. Walking on, you get a cheat's preview of the zoo's Elephant House on the left and an artificial waterfall tumbling to the right. From here, meander along winding paths to the Rose Garden for a quiet, contemplative few moments and then on to Duck Island to see the grey herons roosting there. Close by is the decidedly odd Dummy Tree, a live tree hanging with dummies and symbolizing a local superstition that bringing discarded dummies here

eases a child's path through life. Turn off right here to the Chinese Pavilion (see p 87 for opening times) or continue on to the park's imposing main entrance at Frederiksberg Runddel (it's flooded to form an ice rink in winter) and the equally majestic statue of Frederik VI. *See p 87.*

⑪ ★ Storm P Museet. By the gates of Frederiksberg Have, this tribute to Danish cartoonist and social campaigner Robert Storm Petersen (1882–1949) will bring a wry smile to most faces. Even if you don't understand the cartoons, the drawings are executed with compassion and his collection of pipes is sweetly endearing. ⏱ *30 min. Frederiksberg Runddel.* ☎ *+45 3886 0523. www.stormp-museet.dk. Admission 30DKK, 20DKK seniors and students, free for children under 14. Free with Copenhagen Card. May–Sept Tue–Sun 10am–6pm; Oct–Apr Wed, Sat–Sun 10am–4pm. From here, take bus no 18, 27, or 28 from Frederiksberg Allé or S-tog back to central Copenhagen from Frederiksberg station (turn left down Allégade along the walls of the gardens).*

Chinese Pavillion in Frederiksberg Have.

A Waterfront Walk

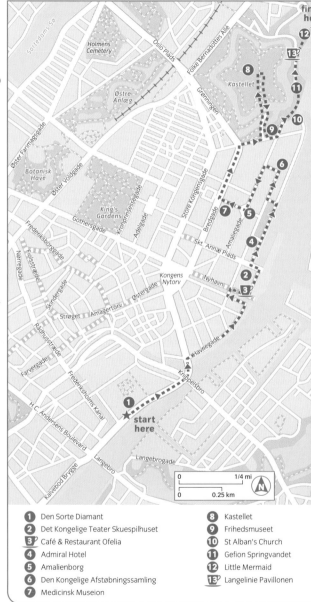

1 Den Sorte Diamant
2 Det Kongelige Teater Skuespilhuset
3 Café & Restaurant Ofelia
4 Admiral Hotel
5 Amalienborg
6 Den Kongelige Afstøbningssamling
7 Medicinsk Museion

8 Kastellet
9 Frihedsmuseet
10 St Alban's Church
11 Gefion Springvandet
12 Little Mermaid
13 Langelinie Pavillonen

Swathes of Copenhagen's 17th-century industrial harbor frontages have all but disappeared, allowing a gleaming new landscape of fabulous buildings to be born. Explore the modern waterfront, see architecture of all periods and styles, visit a couple of oddball museums, and recognize how the maritime commerce that brought the city its wealth is being replaced by the 21st-century industries of leisure and tourism. START: Metro to Kongens Nytorv, 10-minute walk to Black Diamond.

1 ★★★ Den Sorte Diamant (Black Diamond). Spend a happy hour looking at the exhibitions in the Black Diamond; there are often political caricatures in the **Danish Museum of Cartoon Art. The National Museum of Photography** is also well worth your attention; it's elegantly laid out in sleek, minimal spaces and the images exhibited span the history of photography as well as featuring contemporary works. The **Montana Room** is a softly lit circular glass space housing long-term exhibitions. Outside wander around Søren Kierkegård Plads and marvel at the sunlight glinting of the Black Diamond's granite-coated glass façade as it leans over the Øresund. ⏱ *1 hr. Admission free. See p 30, bullet* 4.

2 ★★★ Det Kongelige Teater Skuespilhuset (Royal Danish Playhouse). Walk left along the waterfront, cross under Knippels Bridge, which leads to Christianshavn (see p 63) towards Havnegade, a quiet suburban street with pretty rows of houses leading off. When you hit Nyhavn (see p 7), cross the bridge amid all the hustle and bustle and the wooden boats, grab an ice cream from Vaffelbageren (Nyhavn

Look out for this elephant plaque along the Nyhavn.

The Marmorkirken and Christian IX's Palace in Amalienborg.

49, see p 102) and head for the Royal Danish Playhouse to dangle your feet from the wooden pier. Otherwise it's time to stop off for refreshments at the smart new in-house café, with views across the sound to the Opera House (see p 119). ⏱ *1½ hr if eating. See p 31, bullet ❼. 10-min walk along the waterfront.*

3 ★★ **Café & Restaurant Ofelia.** Mix with the Copenhagen chattering classes over a mint tea or mid-morning coffee. If you get here at lunchtime, it's well worth splashing out on a two-course lunch from the Danish menu. Bag a table by the endless smoked-glass window, kick back, and enjoy the view. *Sankt Annæ Plads 36.* ☎ *+45 3369 6933. www.skuespilhus.dk. $$$.*

4 ★★ **Admiral Hotel.** Just past the square white box of Hotel FRONT (see p 131, with its gorgeous rooms overlooking the sea), the magnificently restored warehouse of the Admiral allows us to see what the Copenhagen waterfront would have looked like in the 1790s; a Copenhagen grown prosperous on overseas trade thanks to its strategic position on the Øresund. The industrial style of the Admiral juxtaposes neatly with the futuristic Opera House over the Øresund and

Floating Sculpture

Just to the left of the Opera House on the opposite side of the Øresund, you'll spot the highlights of my waterfront walk: a series of haunting white sculptures of figures marooned on a pontoon in the middle of the harbor. These were created by recent immigrants from Eastern Europe and apparently symbolize their struggle to settle in Denmark.

the fanciful rococo architecture of the Amalienborg complex beyond. 🕐 *10 min. See p 127. 5 min from Royal Playhouse.*

5 ★★ **Amalienborg.** Continue along the waterfront of Larsens Plads to Christian IX's Palace on the left, the winter residence of Queen Margrethe II and the Prince Consort, and part of a complex of four identical palaces earmarked by the Royal Family as their homes in 1794. Two of these are open to the public, see p 38 for details. If you wash up here at midday, stop off to see the changing of the guard. From the fountain at the entrance to the vast Amalienborg courtyard, the Marmorkirken (see p 42) and the Opera House (see p 119) appear to be exactly in line. Take a couple of minutes among the box hedges of the little gardens of Amaliehaven in front of the palace complex. 🕐 *30 min. See p 41, bullet* **5.** *5-min walk from Admiral.*

6 ★★★ **Den Kongelige Afstøbningssamling (Cast Museum).** The last time I was in Copenhagen, I spotted Ramon Abramovich's massive superyacht *Pelarus* moored outside this eccentric museum; sometimes the Danish Royal Family's yacht can be seen here too. Look for the vast cast of Michelangelo's *David* among the 17th-century warehouses and modern office blocks, some owned by the Danish Navy, which line the waterfront. It was opened in 1895 as a branch of the Statens Museum for Kunst (see p 26) and contains plaster casts taken from over 2,000 famous sculptures dating from classical to Renaissance times. Worth a visit for it's oddball charm although opening hours are restricted to Wednesday and Sunday afternoons. 🕐 *1 hr. Vestindisk Pakhus, Toldbodgade 40. Free admission. Wed 2pm–8pm; Sun 2pm–5pm. Guided tours Mon–Fri 10am–2pm* 📞 *+45 3374 8484, book one week in advance). 10 min along waterfront.*

7 ★★ **Medicinsk Museion (Medical Museum).** Hop round the back of the Cast Museum (see above) to another curiosity, and not one for the faint-hearted. Part repository for the medical collections of the university and part Victorian

Statue of David outside the Cast Museum.

Gefion and her oxes.

horror show, the museum collections feature saws used in early amputations, grisly bits of the human anatomy, and wooden prostheses. A fine lecture hall with domed roof is still in use, and many of the temporary exhibitions aim to educate. 🕐 *1 hr. Bredgade 62.* ☎ *+45 3532 3800. www.mhm.ku.dk. Admission 50DKK, 20DKK seniors and students. Wed–Fri, Sun 1pm–5pm. Guided tours in English at 2.30pm only during Jul and Aug. Behind museum, head towards Bredgade.*

8 ★ **kids** **Kastellet.** If you have kids with you, let them have a romp around in the grounds of this 17th-century star-shaped fortress. There's a windmill to spot and plenty of water birds; herons in particular are often hiding along the moat banks. *See p 16, bullet* **8**. *Opposite end of Bredgade.*

9 ★★★ **Frihedsmuseet (Museum of Danish Resistance).** Turn right on Bredgage, and if you haven't yet visited, stop off a while at my favorite Dansk

Kunstindustri-museet (see p 16) to see decorative arts and design at its apogee. Otherwise, carry on to the Resistance Museum, which relates the story of the Nazi occupation of Denmark between 1940 and 1945. There are photos depicting the hardships suffered by the Danes and the gradual change from acceptance of their lot to resistance movements developing, as well as maps, weapons, uniforms, printing machines for producing underground newspapers, and even a German enigma-code machine. A series of short films features Resistance heroes recounting their experiences. A mock air-raid shelter has been set up just outside the museum, but for me the most touching exhibit was the rose fashioned from chewed bread made by a Polish prisoner in Ravensbrück womens' concentration camp in northern Germany. Part of the Nationalmuseet (see p 9). *Churchillparken 1263.* ☎ *+45 3347 3921. Free admission. Tue–Sat 10am–5pm. In front of Kastellet.*

⑩ ★ St Alban's Church. The 'English church' has a wonderful situation by the side of Kastellet's moat; Copenhagen's only Anglican church was consecrated in 1887 and has an elegant, angular neo-Gothic spire. There are English-speaking services every Sunday at 10.30am. *Churchillparken 6.* ☎ *+45 3962 7736. Close to the Resistance Museum.*

⑪ ★★ Gefion Springvandet (fountain). A step past St Alban's Church, the mythical Gefion is busily ploughing up Swedish soil to claim land for Denmark from King Gylfe; it is said she turned her sons into the four oxen, depicted in this flamboyant bronze with straining backs and flaring nostrils. Designed by Anders Bundgard in 1908, the fountain is built on a slight incline; look straight down for views over Amalienborg (see p 15). *Churchillparken. 10-min photo opportunity. Just up Langelinie, the seafront pathway, from St Alban's Church.*

⑫ ★ kids Little Mermaid. Just beyond Gefion, there is a lookout point on Langelinie with views to the Little Mermaid. Copenhagen's world-famous Little Mermaid sculpture might be small (see p 46) but she's definitely popular—she receives over one million visitors a year to her little boulder with its industrial backdrop. Sadly not everybody is kind to her; her head has been knocked off twice since she was unveiled in 1913. ⏱ *15 min. Langelinie. 10 min from Gefion. From here catch the number 26 bus back into the city center from the shops at Langelinie Allé. 1 hr round walk to and from Bredgade.*

⑬ ★ Langelinie Pavillonen. This glass-fronted pavilion has pole position looking out over the Øresund and its pretty terrace is just the thing for a long, cool lager on summer days. Inside there is an eclectic mix of furniture by design greats, including Arne Jacobsen, and a reasonable buffet menu in the pristine white dining room. *Langelinie 10.* ☎ *+45 3312 1212. eng.langelinie.s-9.dk $$-$$$.*

The Little Mermaid at dusk.

Latin Quarter to Christiania

Today's the day to explore churches and historic buildings in the pedestrianized Latin Quarter and enjoy some interesting shops en route. Later explore a mini-Amsterdam in Christianshavn and leave Denmark altogether in boho Christiania. As always in this compact city, you'll notice the influence of the Danish Royal Family, particularly Christian IV, the king who sought to make Copenhagen the national capital in the 17th century. START: **Bus to Rådhuspladsen.**

1 ★★★ Strøget. I am powerless to walk up this shopping street without being tempted in to some of the stores. Although things are a bit tatty around the Rådhuspladsen, there is plenty of color and some cut-price bargains to be had. Most mornings there is a tiny craft market in Nytorv, where stallholders sell unusual jewelry. It's a square to linger in; sit outside one of the cafés or nose around the adjoining Gammel Torv, with its neoclassical courthouse and imposing Caritas Fountain, the oldest in Copenhagen and built by our good friend Christian IV (see p 167). In warm weather, people sit, drink and picnic on the steps around the fountain. 🕐 *45 min. See p 8.*

2 ★ Vor Frue Kirke. Cut up Nørregade to the Church of Our Lady. Copenhagen's cathedral nave is 60m long and the scene of several royal weddings, including Crown Prince Frederik and Mary Donaldson in 2004. Founded by Bishop Absalon in 1209, this great church has had

Vor Frue Kirke in the Latin Quarter.

a checkered history. Like many medieval Copenhagen buildings, the cathedral burnt down in 1728; its replacement suffered damage under Nelson's siege in 1807, and the present neoclassical version was completed in 1829. The interior is

Five Streets in One

At 1.8km, Europe's longest pedestrianized shopping strip is actually five streets fused into one. Going north from Rådhuspladsen, you hit Frederiksberggade, then Nygade, Vimmelskaftet, Amagertorv, and Østergade before stepping into Kongens Nytorv. The street changes character along the way; around Rådhuspladsen the shops are less expensive and compete for custom with take-away international burger bars. Towards the top end you'll find designer shops and big prices.

Bikes lined up at the University.

chiefly remarkable for the religious statuary by Bertel Thorvaldsen (see p 45), and many visit just to look at the figure of Christ above the altar, with his hands splayed to reveal his stigmata. ⏱ *20 min. Nørregade 8.* ☎ *+ 45 3337 6540. Free admission. Mon–Sat 8am–5pm. 5-min walk up Nørregade from Nytorv.*

❸ ★★ **University Area.** Just behind the cathedral is the site of the university's original campus, founded in 1479 but subsequently damaged in Nelson's siege of the city—much rebuilding took place in the latter half of the 19th century. Although most of the departments have now decamped to shiny new digs at Amager, the law faculty, the library, and a couple of residences remain. The oldest, Regensen, is opposite the Rundetårn, which is itself the university's observatory. The student population is responsible for the multitude of cafés, bookshops, and vintage stores that make this an attractive area to snoop around. ⏱ *45 min. Next to the cathedral.*

❹ ★★ **Paludan Bog & Café.** Opposite the university library, this rambling bookshop (see p 75) has a great café to enjoy delicious hot chocolate and a panini. There are sometimes book readings on Thursday (call to check). *Fiolstræde 10-12.* ☎ *+45 331 0675. www.paludan-bog.dk. $.*

❺ ★★ **Gråbrødretorv.** At the bottom of Fiolstræde, turn left and first right down Klosterstæde into Gråbrødretorv. This pretty square is dominated by a huge plane tree and was once site of a monastery. The 17th-century gabled houses lining the square are attractively painted in bright colors and in the summer the cobbles are covered with tables from restaurants and bars. The best restaurant on the square is the traditional Peder Oxe (see p 99), although the Jensens Bøfhus (Gråbrødretorv 15. ☎ +45 3332 7800) runs a close second, with excellent open sandwiches. The normally low-key square transforms into a buzzing venue during the Copenhagen Jazz

Festival. ⏱ *20 min to wander around, longer if you eat. 5-min walk from Fiolstræde.*

6 ★★★ **Strædet.** Consisting mainly of the two pedestrianized streets of Læderstræde and Kompagnistræde south of Strøget, this chic area of Copenhagen has many shops. I love the piles of silver cutlery and the jewel-colored glassware in the basement windows of the antique shops. Danish womenswear staple wettergren & wettergren (see p 77) and the glamorous vintage shop Kitsch Bitch (see p 82) are two places to head for, as well buying delicate and lacy lingerie at Viola Sky. *Hyskenstræde 16.* ☎ *+45 3315 1815.* ⏱ *1 hr. 5-min walk across Strøget from Gråbrødretorv.*

7 ★ **Slotskirke.** From Læderstræde, walk up to Amagertorv and right across Højbro. Here the Slotskirke forms part of the Christiansborg complex on Slotsholmen, the seat of Danish parliament (see p 39). This squat neoclassical church was designed in 1826 by the classically influenced Danish architect CF Hansen as a mock-Greek temple with pediments and pillars at the entrance. Nowadays it is used for private occasions by the Royal Family and the State Opening of Parliament takes place here every October. Unbelievably the roof burnt down when a firework landed on it in 1992, but Hansen's classical motifs and plasterwork in the interior have all been carefully restored. ⏱ *15 min. Prins Jørgens Gård.* ☎ *+45 3392 6300. Daily July 12pm–4pm; Aug–June Sun 12pm–4pm. 10 min from Strædet.*

8 ★★ **Børsen.** Just past the Slotskirke in the Christianborg complex, the amazing twisted copper tower of the old Stock Exchange (Børsen) sits atop a wonderful Dutch-Baroque gabled civic hall commissioned by Christian IV in 1620 to rival Amsterdam's thriving money markets. Originally it had a similar set-up to an early department store, where anything from grain to household goods could be bought. The hall was built on pillars over the water and is surrounded on three sides by canals, which is probably why this is one of the few old buildings to have survived Copenhagen's frequent fires. The tower is fashioned from four intertwined dragon's tails, while the golden crowns on the spire represent the Nordic powers of Denmark, Sweden, and Norway. ⏱ *10 min. Christiansborg Slotsplads.* ☎ *+45 3395 0500. Not open to public. Visible from Slotskirke.*

9 ★★★ **Christianshavn.** Cross busy Knippels Bridge onto the island of Amager and the trendy, affluent area of Christianshavn, riven with canals packed with moored yachts, motorboats, and houseboats. It doesn't take long to recognize the Dutch influence; the pastel-colored 17th-century canal-side houses are tall and narrow, with gables and crane hooks for pulling goods onto the upper floors. Indeed Christian VI

The gabled Dutch-Baroque Børsen.

Gabled canalside house in Christianshavn.

encouraged Dutch immigrants to settle here in 1619 for their architecture skills, and he later fortified the island with ramparts. I recommend taking half an hour to stroll around the atmospheric streets, in particular Strandgade (first left over the bridge). The minute you leave Torvegade, the main thoroughfare, all is peace and tranquility. ⏱ *1 hr. 5 min over the bridge from Børsen.*

🔟 **★★ Café Wilder.** If you are in need of fortification, there are dozens of cafés and bars around Christianshavn. Café Wilder (see p 95) is a great local option for a sandwich, beer, or glass of wine.

⓫ **★★ Vor Frelsers Kirke.** From Strandgade, take the first right down Sankt Annæ Gade, and cross Christianshavn Kanal to the Church of Our Savior, famed throughout the city for the gilded staircase that runs up the spire and the vast golden globe with a statue of Christ on top. This church is the handiwork of Scandinavian architect Lambert van Haven, who completed its Baroque interior in 1696. Inside, you can't miss the gloriously over-the-top-altar, all flying figures and sunflares, or the massive three-story organ built by the Botzen brothers in 1696–1698 and for once not burnt down or destroyed by Nelson. The wooden spire was added in 1752, more than 50 years after the church was consecrated. Frederik V wanted a landmark tower for Christianshavn and Lauritz de Thurah, the bright light of Danish Baroque architecture, was the man to do this for him. Climb its 400 steps for great views to the city center and the Opera House (see p 119), but it's 90m from the ground to the top of Christ's banner

Houseboats and yachts moored along Christianshavn Kanal.

Mural in Christiania.

and there's not much protection.
🕐 *45 min. Sankt Annæ Gade 29.*
☎ *+ 45 4014 6389.*

⑫ ★ Christiania. Turn left out of Vor Frelsers Kirke and you're in a mini state within the state; Christiania declared its independence from Denmark in the 1970s and has run itself as a separate country since then. People flock here on Sundays for brunch at one of the dozens of restaurants; Spiseloppen at Bådmandsstræde 43 has an ever-changing cuisine delivered by a variety of international chefs. Most visitors come to snoop at Pusher Street, its market stalls and occupants, who take grave exception to being photographed. Plans are afoot to re-integrate Christiania into Copenhagen so that the inhabitants will have to pay Danish taxes!

🕐 *1 hr. From here, have dinner in Christianshavn or catch a performance at the Opera House on Holmen (see p 119), the adjacent island.*

⑬ ★★★ Era Ora. Under the watchful eye of Fabio Donadoni (see p 96), Era Ora is the only Michelin-starred Italian restaurant in Denmark. Deservedly so; the décor is elegant, the terrace overlooks the canal, the wine list well chosen, and the light Italian dishes are a superb treat. *Reservations required. Overgaden Neden Vandet 33B.* ☎ *+45 3254 0693. www.era-ora.dk. $$$.*

The spire of Vor Frelsers Kirke.

Nørrebro & the Lakes

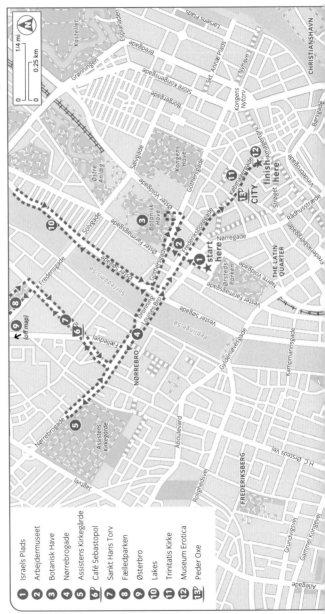

This tour takes you out of the city center to Nørrebro and Østerbro, two distinct areas where 'real' Danish people live, one youthful and laid-back, the other lined with designer shops and expensive housing along wide boulevards. Be warned, there's a lot of walking, so wait for a sunny day and grab your hiking boots. The route encompasses cemeteries, eccentric museums, the odd church, and lots of green spaces. At several points you can break off and return to the city center by bus or S-train. START: **Metro to Nørreport.**

Flowers for sale at the market in Israels Plads.

❶ ★ **Israels Plads.** This huge square is home to a small collection of market stalls selling fruit, vegetables and flowers. In the last few years the market has decreased markedly, with just a few straggling along Frederiksborggade—although the flowers are still enticingly laid out. In fact presently the square seems to be turning into a massive parking lot but this is soon set to change; in mid 2009 a new (largely) organic market opens on the same spot. Pick up organic goodies to consume later and have a root around the stalls. At the time of writing, things are livelier on Saturday, when a flea market spreads its

wares across the square. ⏱ *20 min. Isaels Plads. See p 81.*

❷ ★ **Arbejdermuseet (Workers' Museum).** Just across Frederiksborggade and first right up Rømersgade is an homage to the daily life of the Danish working classes over 170 years. It's hidden away in an historic townhouse built in 1879 and once used as a workers' union building. Permanent exhibitions include displays of machines and processes introduced during industrialization and a somber tableau depicting the struggle of one family during the Depression of 1930s. Proceedings are considerably enlivened by the elegant, balconied assembly hall, where union meetings took place, and even more so by the well-restored beer hall Café & Ølhalle 1892, where there's a good selection of draught and bottled beers, some with original labels from the 1940s. ⏱ *1 hr. Rømersgade 22.* ☎ *+45 3393 2575. Admission 50DKK, 40DKK seniors and students, free for children under 18. Free with Copenhagen Card. Daily 10am–4pm. 5-min walk from Israels Plads.*

❸ ★ **Botanisk Have (Botanical Museum and Gardens).** On a sunny day, wander around the botanical gardens to see what's growing and listen to the ducks squabbling on the lake. If you bought a picnic, settle down on a bench here with views of the Palm House. There's a botanical museum in an elegant red-brick mansion just inside the gardens (entrance at Gothersgade 130); this is not always open, so call ahead to check if this appeals to you. However, anyone with a botanical bent should see if they can get in to view some of the millions of species squirreled away here for research. *See p 86, bullet* ❽. *5-min walk across Gothersgade.*

Classical sculpture at Botanisk Have.

❹ ★★ Nørrebrogade.

For a blast of full-on city life, leave the botanical gardens by the way you came and turn right. Cross over Dronning Louises Bridge, which separates Peblinge Sø and Sortedams Sø, the second and third links in the defensive chain of lakes laid around the western part of the city by Christian IV (see p 168). Straight ahead is Nørrebrogade, pivotal street of down-to-earth and classless Nørrebro. Here students and professionals, people of all nationalities and backgrounds brush along happily. The street is dynamic and buzzing, lined with chain stores, ethnic shops, and supermarkets but it's not without a coating or two of graffiti. ⏱ *30 min. Nørrebrogade. 10-min walk.*

❺ ★ Assistens Kirkegårde.

Past the bustle and noise of Nørrebrogade, I like to seek solace in the tree-lined pathways of this historic cemetery, burial place of philosopher Søren Kirkegård and Hans Christian Andersen (see p 46). Other eminent but less well-known Danes who languish in this quiet corner of Copenhagen include Hans Christian Ørsted, revered for his work in electromagnetism, who passed on in 1851 and lent his name to a pretty park (see p 87) and another, Nobel Prize-winning and somewhat more contemporary physicist, Niels Bohr, who died in 1962. Guided tours of the cemetery are given by tour leaders in period costume; call in advance. There are sometimes concerts in the church and a weekend flea market lays itself out against the walls of the cemetery. *Kapelvej.* ☎ *+45 8233 4640. Free admission. Jan–Feb, Nov–Dec 8am–4pm; Mar–Apr, Sept–Oct 8am–6pm; May–Aug 8am–8pm. Stroll from Nørrebrogade.*

❻ ★ Café Sebastopol.

This Nørrebro institution serves French dishes all day long, with tables and heaters in the square during the summer. I like the big wooden bar for a late-night drink (open until 2am at the weekend). *2 Guldbergsgade, Sankt Hans Torv.* ☎ *+45 3536 3002. www.sebastopol.dk. $$.*

❼ ★★ Sankt Hans Torv.

Meander along Elmegade, taking the time to explore its vibrant cafés and takeaways, bric-à-brac shops and bakeries, to Sankt Hans Torv, acknowledged as Nørrebro's trend-setting heart. All around this edgy square are bars, cafés, vintage shops, and one-off designer boutiques. ⏱ *1 hr. Sankt Hans Torv. 10 min from Assistens Kirkegård.*

❽ ★★ Fælledparken.

Follow Nørre Allé up to Østerbro's largest park, beautifully kept and full of secret pathways; it's a lovely place for a wander among the trees and it's home to Parken (see p 120), where FC København play. There's

The peaceful Fælledparken.

a skate park, soccer fields, cycle lanes, and jogging paths, so if you are feeling energetic one day, this is the place to come and let off steam. ⏲ *30 min. Fælledparken. 15 min from Sankt Hans Torv.*

⑨ ★★★ Østerbro. Cut through **Fælledparken** to Trianglen, with its dumpy, copper-roofed public bathrooms in the middle—known to locals as the 'soup tureen' because of its ungainly shape. If you want to give up here, bus 1A runs back into Kongens Nytorv. At Trianglen, five roads meet to form busy boulevards, the main shopping area of what are considered locally the preserve of 'middle class' Danes, with quality shops like Emmery's (see p 80) and design icon **Normann Copenhagen** worth stopping off for. ⏲ *30 min. Østerbro. 10 min from Fælledparken.*

⑩ ★★ Lakes. On the corner of Østerbrogade and the Lakes, there are a few cafés on the water's edge, which fill to bursting in the summer, especially on weekend lunchtimes, when the wealthy natives of the area are home from work. From here walk down Østerbrogade to skirt through deserted Holmens Kirkegård, with its neat tombs, and

take the path alongside the left of Sortedams Sø to stroll back into the city center. ⏲ *for the walk back into town 50 min.*

⑪ ★★★ Trinitatis Kirke. Cross Gothersgade, and take the next left back along Frederiksborggade to Kultorvet, a city-center piazza full of students and tourists chilling out in pavement bars. Take time out here or carry on to the Rundetårn and its spectacular adjoining church. This typically Danish church, built in

The Lakes by night.

Cherubim and seraphim on the pulpit in Trinitatis Kirke.

1637 at the behest of Christian IV (see p 168), has a painted white interior, exotic carvings on the pulpit, and a flamboyant Baroque altar installed by Friedrich Ehbisch (who also created the altar in Vor Frue Kirke, see p 61) in 1731. *Corner Landemærket 2 / Købmagergade 52A.* ☎ *+45 3337 6540. www.trinitatis kirke.dk. Free admission. Daily 9.30am–4.30pm. A hour's walk along the Lakes from Fælledparken.*

⓬ ★ **Museum Erotica.** Guaranteed to bring a snigger to most lips, this museum opens until late into the evening and it's just round the corner from the Rundetårn—a lighthearted way to wind up a long day. In my experience if you do go in late at night, you'll be accompanied by bands of tittering half-drunk stag nighters from the UK, Sweden, or Germany, so perhaps pay a visit before supper. In a remarkably ornate setting with painted ceilings, this is a whistle-stop tour through our innermost desires through paintings, sculpture, magazines, and yes, sex toys too. There's also an informative section about the pornography industry in Denmark, which was legalized in 1967. *Købmagergade 24.* ☎ *+45 3312 0311. www.museumerotica.dk. Adm 100DKK, students 65DKK. Oct–Apr Sun–Thur 11am–8pm, Fri 10am–12am, Sat 10am–9pm; May–Sept daily 10am–10pm.*

⓭ ★★★ **Peder Oxe.** There are so many food choices in the pedestrianized city center. Try Peder Oxe (see p 99) as a special treat—perfect for a last nostalgic Danish dinner in Copenhagen, or any of the cafés of Kultorvet (see above), although this is quite a touristy area and prices will reflect that. If you are up for a long evening of Danish hospitality (*hygge*), head for the bars and restaurants of Nyhavn, a 15-minute walk away. *Gråbrødretorv 11.* ☎ *+45 3311 0077. www.pederoxe. dk. Open daily.* ●

Copenhagen Shopping

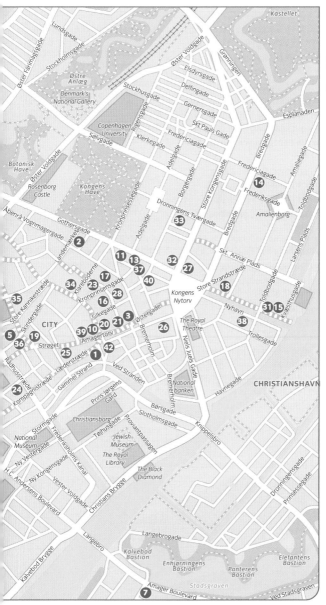

Shopping Best Bets

Longest Shopping Street
★★ *Strøget. (p 78)*

Best One-Stop Shopping
★★★ Illum, *Østergade 52. (p 77)*

Biggest Shopping Mall
★★ Field's, *Arne Jacobsens Allé 12. (p 81)*

Best Silversmith
★★★ Georg Jensen, *Amagertorv 4. (p 82)*

Best Hand-Blown Glass
★★★ Nyhavns Glaspusteri, *Toldbodgade 4. (p 75)*

Best Colorful Copenhagen Design
★★★ Illums Bolighus, *Amagertorv 10. (p 78)*

Best-selling Souvenirs
★ House of Amber, *Kongens Nytorv 2. (p 79)*

Best Antiques
★★★ Hanne Rasmussen, *Nyhavn 65. (p 75)*

Best Up-and-Coming Jewelry Designer
★★★ Green Door, *Grønnegade 43. (p 81)*

Prettiest Household Design Shop
★★ Hanne Gundelach, *Bredgade 56. (p 80)*

Best Leader of the Fashion Pack
★★★ munthe plus simonsen, *Grønnegade 10. (p 77)*

Most Extravagant Shoes
★★★ Perla, *Grønnegade 41a. (p 82)*

Best Mad Hatter
★★ Modist Susanne Juul, *Store Kongensgade 14. (p 77)*

Best Retro Clothing
★★ Kitsch Bitch, *Læderstræde 30. (p 82)*

Best Kids' Boutique
★★ Óli Prik, *St Kongensgade 7. (p 76)*

Best Organic Coffee
★★ Verde Food and Coffee, *Nørre Farimagsgade 72. (p 80)*

Best Chocolatier
★★★ Summerbird, *Ny Østergade 9. (p 75)*

Best New Gourmet Kid on the Block
★★★ Nimb, *Bernstoffsgade 5. (p 80)*

Best Place to Buy a Picnic
★★★ Emmery's, *Vesterbrogade 34. (p 80)*

Best Beer Sommelier
★★ BarleyWine, *Læderstræde 16. (p 82)*.

Beautifully packaged chocolates in Summerbird.

Copenhagen Shopping A to Z

Antiques & Art

★★ GB Antiques TIVOLI   A vast emporium crammed with blue-and-white Royal Copenhagen pottery, kitsch Bing and Grøndhal porcelain figurines, cutlery sets, collectible silver and Little Mermaid plates. Not the most sophisticated antiques shop, but reasonable and well situated close to Tivoli (see p 10). *Ved Glyptotek 6.* ☎ *+45 2168 2529. www.gb-antiques. com. MC, V. Bus 2A, 5A, 15. Map p 72.*

★★★ Hanne Rasmussen NYHAVN Lovely little shop hidden away in a buckled old house at the quiet end of Nyhavn, selling affordable and colorful period glassware, model boats and some typically Danish painted wooden furniture. *Nyhavn 65.* ☎ *+45 3393 3777. MC, V. Metro: Kongens Nytorv. Map p 72.*

★★★ Nyhavns Glaspusteri NYHAVN   Beautiful hand-blown glass in clean, pure lines and bright tones. Everything is created on site by artist Christian Edwards; watch him at work and buy a set of jewel-tinted *schnapps* glasses to take home. *Toldbodgade 4.* ☎ *+45 3313 0134. www.copenhagenglass.dk. AE, MC, V. Metro: Kongens Nytorv. Map p 72.*

Books

★★ Paludan Bog & Café LATIN QUARTER   Across the road from the university library, this is the preferred haunt of student bookworms.

Second-hand books, DVDs, and CDs are on the ground floor, with an extensive collection of fiction and coffee-table books upstairs. There's a little café in which to enjoy a mid-morning pastry while reading your purchases and a stall of old books along the library wall for students to rummage through. *Fiolstræde 10–12.* ☎ *+45 3315 0675. www.paludan-bog.dk. MC, V. Metro: Nørreport. Map p 72.*

Cakes & Chocolate

★★★ kids Conditoriet La Glace STRØGET   Copenhagen's oldest confectioners has been making lacey, layered cakes, pastries, chocolates and ice cream since 1870. Sample the goodies in the elegant two-story café or bag a box of buttery cookies

Copenhagen's oldest confectioners—La Glace.

for lunch in the Kongens Have (see p 86). *Skoubogade 3-5.* ☎ *+45 3314 4646. www.LaGlace.com. MC, V. Metro: Kongens Nytorv. Map p 72.*

★★★ PB Chokolade STRØGET Right next door to Conditoriet La Glace (see above), the Bagger family have turned chocolate into a modern art form. Buy a selection of champagne truffles and multi-flavored pyramid- and heart-shaped chocs—the perfect present for back home. *Skoubogade 1.* ☎ *+45 3393 0717. www.franskemandler.dk. MC, V. Metro: Kongens Nytorv. Map p 72.*

★★★ Summerbird STRØGET A fine range of simply packaged and truly delicious liqueur chocolates,

Build-a-Bear, close to Tivoli.

spreads, marzipan bars, petit fours, gift boxes, and organic bars. They're pricey (the organic chocolate is reputedly the most expensive in the world) but they're worth it! *Ny Østergade 9.* ☎ *+45 3313 1902. www.summerbird.dk. AE, MC, V. Metro: Kongens Nytorv. Map p 72.*

Children
★★ kids Build-a-Bear TIVOLI Kids get to design their favorite bear or bunny, stuff them, dress them up, and take them home. You get to pay handsomely for this, but it's worth it to see their enraptured faces. Cleverly placed by the main entrance to Tivoli to lure you in while standing in line for tickets. *Store Vesterbrogade 3.* ☎ *+45 3313 8030. www.buildabear. dkAE, DC, MC, V. Bus: 2A, 5A, 15. Map p 72.*

★★ kids Óli Prik FREERIKSSTADEN Quite the prettiest children's shop in town. There are delicate smocked dresses in pastel shades for little princesses and cute striped shirts in softest linen for the boys. Few can resist the floppy-eared knitted rabbits, wooden jigsaws, and pastel-colored crocheted blankets. *Store Kongensgade 7.* ☎ *+45 3315 1593. www.oliprik.dk. AE, MC, V. Metro: Kongens Nytorv. Map p 72.*

China
★★★ Royal Copenhagen STRØGET Royal Copenhagen's famous blue-and-white patterned china sells at a remarkable rate from a wondrous gabled shop on Strøget. If you are shocked by the price tags on the Flora Danica pieces, have a look at the reasonably priced seconds in the basement. *Amagertorv 6.* ☎ *+45 3313 7181. www.royal copenhagen.com. AE, DC, MC, V. Metro: Kongens Nytorv. Map p 72.*

Department Stores
★★ Birger Christensen STRØGET Sleek, cool, and expensive, this is the flagship shop of Copenhagen's poshest chain of shops. Men's concessions include Viktor and Rolf and Balenciaga, but the real strength is the acres of women's fashions, including English

label Katharine Hamnett, Prada, Miu Miu, and the casual clothes of Juicy Couture. *Østergade 38.* ☎ *+45 3311 5555. www.birger-christensen.com. AE, DC, MC, V. Metro: Kongens Nytorv. Map p 72.*

★★★ **Illum** STRØGET Expertly laid out to highest Danish design ideals, exclusive Illum leads the way in Copenhagen for designer clothes (Acne Jeans, Ralph Lauren, Diesel, and Paul Smith), cosmetics, expensive jewelry, and quality accessories. *Østergade 52.* ☎ *+45 3314 4002. www.illum.eu. AE, DC, MC, V. Metro: Kongens Nytorv. Map p 72.*

★ **Magasin du Nord** STRØGET You'll find a quality Mad & Vin supermarket alongside a Meyers deli, clothing and accessories, household goods and a bookshop. Housed in an enormous and recently revamped building first opened in 1868. *Kongens Nytorv 13.* ☎ *+45 3311 4433. www.magasin.dk. AE, DC, MC, V Metro: Kongens Nytorv. Map p 72.*

Designer Clothes & Accessories

★★★ **Holly Golightly** KONGENS NYTORV This on-trend boutique flogs top labels from Balenciago and Marni to Marc Jacobs. Luxury leather accessories can be found in the Store Regnegade branch. *Gammel Mønt 2.* ☎ *+45 3314 1915. Also at: Store Regnegade 2.* ☎ *+45 3314 1911. www.hollygolightly.dk. AE, MC. V. Metro: Kongens Nytorv. Map p 72.*

★★ **Modist Susanne Juul** FREDERIKSSTRADEN Neat stylish headwear, fluffy angora berets, and felt pill box hats from one of Copenhagen's newest talents. She also sells elegant gloves in bright colors and the softest leather, made by Randers Handsker. *Store Kongensgade 14.* ☎ *+45 3332 2522. www.susannejuul.dk. MC, V. Metro: Kongens Nytorv. Map p 72.*

★★★ **munthe plus simonsen** STRØGET A Danish design leader and a favorite among supermodels. Spacious and calm, this boutique is hidden away in an attractive courtyard and always manages to keep one step ahead of its rivals. The clothes are glam and superbly made; the prices reflect this. *Grønnegade 10.* ☎ *+45 3332 0312. www. munthneplussimonsen.com. AE, MC, V. Metro: Nørreport. Map p 72.*

★★ **wettergren & wettergren** STRÆDET In this cluttered basement store with tiny fitting rooms, you'll find staples for every woman's wardrobe, from classic white linen shirts to well-cut trousers and ladylike skirts. *Læderstræde 5.* ☎ *+45 3313 1405. AE, MC, V. Metro: Kongens Nytorv. Map p 72.*

Design Shops

★★ **Hay Cph** LATIN QUARTER The ultimate in street design with minimalist furniture created by contemporary greats Jakob Wagner, Louise Campbell, and Hay's own design studio. Bright and funky carpets mix and match with quirky household accessories in edgy colors. *Pilestræde*

Leading designers for women at munthe plus simonsen.

Elegant glassware at Illums Bolighus.

surroundings. Lighting designed by the great Arne Jacobsen (see p 169) sits alongside products by Hay Studio and trendy white china and glassware from Normann Copenhagen (see below). *Amagertorv 10.* ☎ *+45 3314 1941. www.illums bolighus.com. AE, DC, MC, V. Metro: Kongens Nytorv. Map p 72.*

★★ **Kartell** LATIN QUARTER An homage to minimalist design; chairs, stools, glassware by Philippe Starck, lampshades in garish colors, and transparent plastic tables. Still considered a design leader, but I think it's all looking a bit dated. *Kristen Bernikowsgade 6.* ☎ *+45 3393 1931. www,kartell.it. E, MC, V. Metro: Nørreport. Map p 72.*

★★★ **Normann Copenhagen** ØSTERBRO Relative newcomer to the vibrant Copenhagen design scene, this is a true lifestyle emporium selling everything from clothes

29–31. ☎ *+45 9942 4400. www.hay. dk. MC, V. Metro: Nørreport. Map p 72.*

★★★ **Illums Bolighus** STRØGET Copenhagen's favorite interiors' store sells contemporary and accessible Danish design in elegant

On-Trend Shopping Streets

Copenhagen's compact heart is neatly dissected by **Strøget**, the longest pedestrianized shopping street in Europe (see p 8), which connects the tourist hotspots of Nyhavn and Tivoli. Towards Rådhuspladsen the boutiques are predominantly high-street chains, with shops becoming progressively smarter heading north towards **Kongens Nytorv**, where you'll find top-end labels Gucci, Chanel, Bottega Veneta, Cartier as well as Birger Christensen (the Danish equivalent of Browns in London), Georg Jensen (see p 82) and the Royal Copenhagen flagship store (see p 76). Nearby the streets of **Læderstræde** and **Kompagnistræde** are full of independent designers and basement shops crammed with silver and glassware. **Grønnegade** has a selection of upscale independent fashion stores, while galleries and museum-quality antique shops line decorous **Store Kongensgade** and **Bredegade**. Gritty Istedgade in **Vesterbro** is shaking off its seamy image to become home to funky clothing boutiques, a hotchpotch of multi-national restaurants, bars, and gourmet food shops. Trendy **Nørrebro** is the place for second-hand finds along Birkegade and Elmegade, while many Copenhageners do their weekly shopping on the wide boulevards of **Østerbro**.

Port Nouveau Erik Buch on the shady, western side of Nyhavn.

by Acne and Noir to glassware by Marcel Wanders. Located in an ex-sound studio flooded with white light and display stands. *Østerbrogade 70.* ☎ *+45 3555 4459. www.normann-copenhagen.com. AE, MC, V. Bus 4A. Map p 72.*

Flowers

★★ Bering Flowers LATIN QUARTER Spectacular one-off arrangements in pretty glass vases, wedding flowers, roses in baskets, and exquisite table decorations. There are lots of unusual vases and candles for sale as well. Staff will deliver to some of the larger hotels. *Landemærket 12.* ☎ *+45 3315 2611. www.bering flowers.com. AE, MC, V. Metro: Nørreport. Map p 72.*

★★★ Port Nouveau Erik Buch NYHAVN In a 17th-century house on the quiet side of Nyhavn, Erik Buch creates spectacular flower arrangements for all occasions, and in the past, this has included bouquets for Queen Margrethe. There are also decorative wooden boxes and candlesticks on sale; visit the shop for the sheer visual experience. *Nyhavn 12.* ☎ *+45 3254 2088. www.erikbuch.dk. MC, V. Metro: Kongens Nytorv. Map p 72.*

Gifts

★★ Girlie Hurly VESTERBRO A confection of feminine, pink household gifts; purple vases, crimson lamp stands, Moroccan glasses, patterned straw baskets, pretty smocked tops. *Istedgade 101.* ☎ *+45 3324 2241. www.girliehurly.dk. MC. V. Bus: 2A, 5A, 216. Map p 72.*

★ House of Amber NYHAVN With the high quality of the wares guaranteed by the adjacent Museum of Amber, this shop is full to the gills with dramatic amber jewelry set in

Girlie Hurly is a favorite stop for feminine birthday treats.

Inviting courtyard at Hanne Gundelach.

gold and silver or studded with diamonds. Not the cheapest of souvenirs, but certainly the most beautiful. There are four other stores in the city center. *Kongens Nytorv 2.* ☎ *+45 3311 6700. www.houseof amber.com. AE, DC, MC, V. Metro: Kongens Nytorv. Map p 72.*

Gourmet & Organic Food
★★★ Emmery's VESTERBRO
For high quality and often organic breads, sandwich fillings, coffees, teas, and wines, head to one of the nine branches of Emmery's, some of which have small cafés attached. A great stop-off for picnic fodder. *Vesterbrogade 34.* ☎ *+45 3322 7763. www.emmerys.dk. MC, V. Bus: 2A, 5A, 216. Map p 72.*

★★★ Nimb TIVOLI Occupying the Moorish palace at Tivoli (see p 10), Nimb is a gastronomic paradise with an organic dairy, chocolate factory, and deli featuring foods from Summerbird (see p 75) and Løgismose (a great Danish deli institution with a branch in Østerbro). *Bernstoffsgade 5.* ☎ *+45 8870 0060. www.nimb.dk. AE, MC, V. Bus: 2A, 5A, 15. Map p 72.*

★★ Ostehjørnet FRED-
ERIKSSTADEN An old-fashioned purveyor of fine cheese and great

slabs of salami. Divine foodie smells will entice you in! *Store Kongensgade 56.* ☎ *+45 3315 5011. www. ostehjoernet.dk. AE, MC, V. Metro: Kongens Nytorv. Map p 72.*

★★ Verde Food and Coffee
NØRREPORT Rather a mundane-looking shop but one that sells all your organic requisites from shampoos to peanut butter and flower-infused cosmetics. Sample an iced coffee or fresh juice (both organic, of course) and catch up on your emails on one of the Macs in the window for 30DKK per hour. *Nørre Farimagsgade 72.* ☎ *+45 7020 3015. Verde.dk. AE, MC, V. Metro: Nørreport. Map p 72.*

Household Design
★★★ Georg Jensen Damask
STRØGET A treasure trove of luxurious damask tablecloths, towels, kimonos and bed linen in all shades from anthracite to the purest white. No relation of Georg Jensen the silversmith (see p 82). *Dieselvej 1.* ☎ *+45 7552 2700. www.georg jensen.com AE, DC, MC, V. Metro: Kongens Nytorv. Map p 72.*

★★ Hanne Gundelach FRED-
ERIKSSTADEN Ethnic sculptures, massive Chanukah candlesticks, giant planters, and tinkling indoor fountains make this one of Copenhagen's most

eclectic interior-design stores. It is tucked away in a little cobbled square behind the Medical Museum (see p 57). *Bredgade 56. ☎ +45 3311 3396. www.gundelach.dk. AE, MC, V. Metro: Kongens Nytorv. Map p 72.*

★★ **Kif Kif** STRÆDET All things Moroccan; here you'll find brightly patterned woven rugs with shaggy fringes, soft leather stools in warm colors, tea services, mirrors with tooled glass frames, and wrought-ironwork furniture. There is also an interior design service providing soft furnishings and home decorating. *Kompagnistræde 30. ☎ +45 3535 8855. www.kifkif.dk. MC, V. Metro: Kongens Nytorv. Map p 72.*

Jewelry
★★★ **Green Door** STRØGET Features the extraordinary jewelry of Susanne Friis Bjørner, who sells her work worldwide. Some pieces are reminiscent of Bronze Age torques fashioned out of flattened gold links, others have stars dangling on huge hooped silver earrings, and bracelets with heart-shaped semi-precious stones. *Grønnegade 43. ☎ +45 3312 3636. www.greendoor.dk. MC, V. Metro: Kongens Nytorv. Map p 72.*

★★ **P Hertz** STRØGET Jewelers to the Danish Court, P Hertz has been selling traditional designs since 1834; it is very much the place where Copenhageners buy their engagement and wedding rings. Any design can be created in their workshop. *Købmagergade 34. ☎ +45 3312 2216. www.phertz.dk. MC, V. Metro: Nørreport. Map p 72.*

Mall
★★ kids **Field's** ØRESTAD Ten minutes out of town by train or metro, Copenhagen's mammoth shopping center has 140 shops, including benchmark stores Bilka OneStop Hypermarket, El Gigantre

(electronics) and Magasin, with international brand concessions. Level 2 is where you'll find the cafés and restaurants as well as fun golf for junior shoppers, a fitness center, and a large play area for toddlers. *Arne Jacobsens Allé 12. ☎ +45 7020 8505. www.fields.dk. AE, DC, MC, V. Metro: Ørestad. Map p 72.*

Markets
★ **Israels Plads** NØRREPORT Currently site of a small daily fruit, vegetable, and flower market. A vast new and largely organic grocery market called Torvehallerne is scheduled to open here in mid 2009. There is also a Saturday flea market in the square. *Israels Plads. Metro: Nørreport. Map p 72.*

★★ **Frederiksberg Flea Market** FREDERIKSBERG Copenhagen's poshest flea market runs on Sunday from April to October. Get down to this affluent district of town early for the chance to pick up a bargain or two, although you will find more designer clothing than antiques. Parking lot behind City Hall. *☎ +45 3819 2142, ext. 4016. www.frederiksberg.dk/loppetorv. No Credit Cards. Metro: Frederiksberg. Map p 72.*

A flower stall in Israels Plads.

Shopping Know-How

Copenhagen operates fairly standard shop opening times; typical hours are Monday to Friday 9.30am to 5.30 or 6.30pm, Saturday 9am to 3 or 4pm. Sunday shopping is still surprisingly limited by law to 23 days a year, usually the first Sunday of each month, although a few food stores and many tourist shops in the center of town choose to stay open on summer Sundays.

- Sales are held twice annually, in late December/early January for two weeks, and again a fortnight in July/August.
- For information on sales tax and related rebates for non-EU residents, see p 166.

Shoes

★★★ Perla KONGENS NYTORV This small shop sells the most fabulously over-the-top shoes adorned with Hello Kitty! logos, pearly buttons, buckles, sparkly colors, and frills. *Grønnegade 41a.* ☎ *+45 3332 0520. MC, V. Metro: Kongens Nytorv. Map p 72.*

★★ Hr Sko LATIN QUARTER Tucked away in a charming little arcade, this has the widest range of men's shoes in Copenhagen, be it an expensive pair of brogues or Timberland boots. *Jorcks Passage, Vimmelskaftet 42B.* ☎ *+45 3315 3222. MC, V. Metro: Kongens Nytorv. Map p 72.*

Silverware

★★★ Georg Jensen STRØGET Quality cutlery, gold and silver decorative arts and handcrafted jewelry can be obtained from this beautiful shop. Downstairs a museum shows seminal silverwork from 1904 to 1940, including Henning Koppel's famous Platypus Dish, as well as exhibits from the original Daisy Collection of jewelry designed by Georg Jensen himself. *Amagertorv 4.* ☎ *+45 3311 4080. www. georgjensen.com. AE, DC, MC, V. Metro: Kongens Nytorv. Map p 72.*

Vintage

★ Kitsch Bitch STRÆDET An alluring collection of retro clothing featuring vintage 1950s' dresses, retro 1970s' kitchenware and piles of love beads, bangles, and dangly earrings. Guys are catered for with shirts, Levi jeans, and trainers. *Læderstræde 30.* ☎ *+45 3313 6313. MC, V. Metro: Kongens Nytorv. Map p 72.*

Wine & Beer Merchant

★★ BarleyWine STRÆDET With fine wines, champagnes, and handmade chocolates on offer, the major selling point here is the expertise of Jan Filipe, Copenhagen's premier beer sommelier. There are beers from Danish micro-breweries, Belgian beers (Trappist and Weissbier), English stouts, and even a few US labels. *Læderstræde 16.* ☎ *+45 3391 9397. www.barleywine.dk. AE, MC, V. Metro: Kongens Nytorv. Map p 72.* ●

Copenhagen **Outdoors**

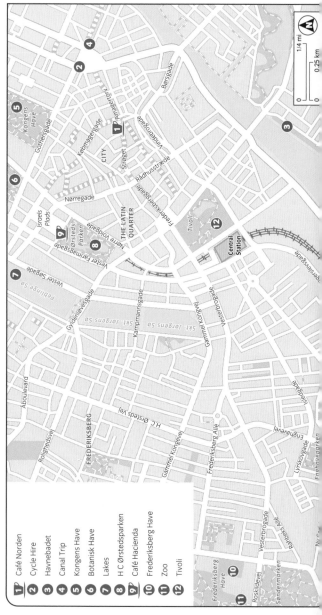

1. Café Norden
2. Cycle Hire
3. Havnebadet
4. Canal Trip
5. Kongens Have
6. Botanisk Have
7. Lakes
8. H C Ørstedsparken
9. Café Hacienda
10. Frederiksberg Have
11. Zoo
12. Tivoli

1/4 mi
0.25 km

Central Station

Tivoli

THE LATIN QUARTER

CITY

Strøget

Nørregade

FREDERIKSBERG

Kongens Have

Israels Plads

Ørsteds Parken

Frederiksberg Have

Peblinge Sø

Skt Jørgens Sø

Sankt Jørgens Sø

Gothersgade

Købmagergade

Amagertorv

Vindebrogade

Borgsgade

Rådhusstræde

Frederiksberggade

Nørre Voldgade

Vester Farimagsgade

Vester Søgade

Gyldenløvesgade

Kampmannsgade

Gammel Kongevej

Vesterbrogade

Åboulevard

Rolighedsvej

H C Ørsteds Vej

Gammel Kongevej

Frederiksberg Allé

Vesterbrogade

Roskildevej

Sandermarken

Randers Allé

Lyrskovgade

Enghaveyej

Istedgade

Ingerslevsgade

Enghaveparken

Being a compact city, I anticipated Copenhagen being intensely urbanized. In fact it is a surprisingly green, outdoors sort of city, with vast areas of parkland and water. Cyclists throng the streets, sunbathers, joggers and walkers crowd the huge landscaped royal parks, cafés spill on to the streets and yachts pack the Øresund in summer. What follows is a series of outdoor experiences by bike to make for a satisfying day in the saddle. START: **Metro to Kongens Nytorv.**

Café Norden.

1 ★★ **Café Norden.** Only early birds get a table outside this prime Strøget meeting place but it's worth the scramble for delicious smoked salmon salads and chocolate cake to follow. *Østergade 61.* ☎ *+45 3311 7791. www.cafenorden.dk. $$.*

2 ★★★ kids **Cycle Hire.** Copenhagen has truly embraced this green trend with ample cycle lanes and easy access to bike hire. Between April and November, pick up a free city bike (with a refundable 20DKK deposit) from one of over 100 racks all over town. For today, pick up your bike in Kongens Nytorv. From here there are a couple of route choices. *Bike hire: Baisikeli, 90–120DKK for 24 hours, www.cph-bike-rental.dk. Free bikes: Bycyklen København, www.bycyklen.dk.*

3 ★★ kids **Havnebadet.** If Copenhagen's uncertain summer temperatures are high, cycle down Niels Juels Gade and Christians Brygge and over Langerbro to Islands Brygge. Here spend the day with sun worshippers at a man-made harbor pool. Grab a deckchair, swim in the pristine waters, or join a game of volleyball. *Havnebadet: Islands*

Wintertime Fun

Copenhagen's grandest square is flooded to form an ice rink in the winter months with skate hire available per hour (inclusive of an hour's skating fee). Afterwards, recovering skaters can unwind with a mulled wine (gløgg) at a Nyhavn bar. Kongens Nytorv. ⏲ *1 hr. Nov 12–Mar 4 Mon–Fri 12pm–10pm; Sat–Sun 10am–10pm. (40DKK per hour skate hire). Metro to Kongens Nytorv.*

Canal boat tour heading away from Kongens Nytorv along Nyhavn.

Brygge. ☎ +45 2371 3189. Daily early June–late Aug 11am–7pm. Water taxi or canal cruise from Gammel Strand or Nyhavn.

④ ★★★ **kids** **Canal Trip.** There are three hop-on, hop-off waterbus routes (green, orange and blue) to explore, sailing between the Little Mermaid (see p 59) and Fisketorvet, with four stops on the way. There are multi-language guided tours available—check website for details. *www.canaltours.com. See p 7 for booking details and timetables.*

⑤ ★★ **kids** **Kongens Have (King's Gardens).** If the weather is not so bright, go straight up Gothersgade to Denmark's oldest royal park. The King's Gardens surround Rosenborg Slot (castle, see p 20) and date back to 1606; they are dotted with sculpture, including a well-loved figure of storyteller H C Andersen (see p 45). Danish families come here in

their thousands to relax, stroll with prams, meet up with friends, and enjoy the summer sunshine. The herbaceous borders, rose gardens, and herb beds are reminiscent of Luxembourg Gardens in Paris. Stop off if you wish to explore the castle. ⏱ *2 hrs. Øster Voldgade 4A.* ☎ *+45 3315 3286. www.rosenborgslot.dk. Daily. Metro: Nørreport. Bus 6a, 184, 185, 180S, 173E.*

⑥ ★ **Botanisk Have (Botanical Gardens).** Across Øster Volgade is another of Copenhagen's green havens; a botanical garden and part of the Natural History Museum of Denmark. Spend a couple of hours in the thyme- and mint-scented grounds, cultivated with around 15,000 species of plant. Stretch out by the ornamental lake or climb the stairs to the top of the rotund Palm House (open May–Sept 10am–3pm) reminiscent of the palm house in London's Kew Gardens. For those with a great interest in fungi and plant life, there is a botanical museum by the main entrance. ⏱ *2 hrs. Gothersgade 128.* ☎ *+45 3532 2220. botanik.snm.ku.dk. Summer daily 8.30am–6pm; winter Tue–Sun 8.30am–4pm.*

⑦ ★ **Lakes.** Continue up Gothersgade for the three artificial lakes separating the city center from Østerbro and Nørrebro. Built as part of Christian IV's (see p 167) defence system guarding the western edge of the city in the 16th century, they were later used as reservoirs. In 1959 they were commandeered by joggers and walkers, and now provide a peaceful respite with a smattering of cafés around the banks. Snooze in summer sunshine on a bench overlooking Sortedams Sø, or watch the swans bob among the pedalos and boats for hire. ⏱ *1-2hrs walk. Sankt Jørgens Sø, Peblinge Sø, Sortedams Sø. Metro to Nørreport or Østerbro.*

8 ★ **H C Ørstedsparken.** A hop from the Lakes, this delightful little park was once part of the same defence system and is named after famous Danish scientist and inventor H C Ørsteds. Created in 1879, there are rural vistas among the relaxed English-style landscaping and pathways dotted with classical statues. Local children pack the playground at the north end of the lake. At night the park becomes a cruising haunt. 🕐 *40 min. Nørre Voldgade.* ☎ *+45 3315 7875. Dawn–dusk daily. Metro: Nørreport.*

9 kids **Café Hacienda.** Great views over the lake in the Ørstedsparken. Get there early for a lunchtime seat on the terrace and a simple selection of *smørrebrød*; if you have worked up a thirst, sample a pint of dry Swedish cider. *Nørre Farimagsgade 6.* ☎ *+45 3333 8533. $.*

Sculpture in H.C. Ørstedsparken.

10 ★★★ kids **Frederiksberg Have (gardens).** A 25-minute pedal down Vesterbrogade brings cyclists to the elegant boulevard of Frederiksberg Allé. This leads to the

Get Out of Town

Once a royal hunting ground, **Dyrehaven** boasts a splendid 16th-century hunting lodge high on a hill overlooking the estate. Pack a picnic from **Ostehjørnet** (see p 80) and head off to spot deer roaming free in leafy cultivated woodland 10km north of Copenhagen. Trot around the park by horse-drawn carriage; you'll find them for hire just inside the red entrance gates. 🕐 *3 hrs. 2930 Klampenborg.* ☎ *+45 3997 3900. Train: S-Train to Klampenborg or 20-minute drive along the coast road E152.*

Alternatively, slip anchor and head out into the **Øresund** early in the morning for a perfect day's sailing in sheltered waters. My favorite escape from Copenhagen is to head to the tiny Swedish island of Ven (spelt Hven in Danish). The 16th-century home to moustachioed astronomer Tycho Brahe has been developed in recent years. There are lots of yacht-charter companies around but JS have the most routes and new boats. *JS Boatcharter, Brobergsgade 1.* ☎ *+45 3296 9016. www.js-boatcharter.dk.*

Cycling in the City

If you decide to take a free hire bike for the day, stay within the confines of the city—from the east side of the Lakes to Christianshavn, and from the docks in the north south to Vesterbrø just behind the station. Otherwise there is a chance of the police fining you. Some family-orientated trips include a ride along the esplanade of Langelinie (see p 17) to visit the Little Mermaid (see p 59) or fit families may prefer the 5km cycle to Amager Beach for a paddle in the sea. You can always get the metro back from the beach, at no extra charge for the bike.

sweeping park of Frederiksberg Have, which feels like a local secret. Designed in French classical style with English landscaping, pathways lead here and there past a Chinese pavilion (open Sun May 1–Sept 1, straight on from the main gates), ornamental lakes and fountains, and even a Greek temple. Dominating all the follies is a real palace—austere Frederiksberg Slot (castle, see p 52). Combine a walk or cycle here with a visit to the zoo (see below). *Frederiksberg Runddel 1a. www.ses.dk. Daily 6am–9pm.*

Frederiksberg Have—where everyone goes on sunny days.

⑪ ★★ kids Zoo. Cycle through the gardens and join massive lines of up to an hour to enjoy the open-air animal enclosures; see hippos paddling around underwater and giraffes thoughtfully chewing hay. A big attraction is the soaring glass span of the Norman Foster elephant house erected in 2008. ⏱ *2 hrs. Roskildevej 38.* ☎ *+45 7220 0285. www.zoo.dk. Admission 130DKK, 70DKK children 3–11. Nov–Mar daily 9am–4pm; Apr–May, Sep–Oct daily 9am–5pm; June 1–27, Aug 18–31 daily 9am–6pm; June 28–Aug 31 daily 9am–9pm. One hour later at weekends except June 28–Aug 31. Bus 6A.*

⑫ ★★★ kids Tivoli by night. It's back to Tivoli to round off a long day with some night-time jollity. Two million fairy lights make Tivoli come to life at night; kids mob the 25 fairground rides—one for every age and nerve—plus the tacky arcades, hot dog stands, and aquarium. You could visit time and time again to sample the 43 restaurants and cafés and roam the ornamental gardens twinkling with Japanese lanterns. Inaugurated in 1843, Tivoli's magical gardens cover six hectares and entertain 4.5 million visitors (mostly Danes) each year. *See p 10 for details.* ●

The Best Dining

Copenhagen Dining

Dining Best Bets

Most Spectacular Waiting Staff
★★★ Peder Oxe $$$ *Gråbrødretorv 11.* (p 99)

Best Smushi
★★★ The Royal Café $$ *Amagertorv 6.* (p 100)

Best Pickled Herring
★★★ Café Petersborg $$ *Bredgade 76.* (p 94)

Best Thai Food on Board a Boat
★★ Mai Thai $$ *Docktorget 1, Malmö.* (p 102)

Best Fresh Seafood in Nyhavn
★★ Cap Horn $$$ *Nyhavn 21.* (p 96)

Best Michelin Starred Organic Restaurant
★★★ Geranium $$$$$ *Kronprinsessegade 13.* (p 97)

Best Trendy Restaurant with a Vietnamese Menu
★★★ Lê Lê $$$ *Vesterbrogade 40.* (p 98)

All on board for a Thai meal at Mai Thai in Malmö.

Most Beautiful Café
★★ Café Glyptotek $$$ *Dantes Plads 7.* (p 93)

Favorite Haunt of Hans Christian Andersen
★★ Café à Porta $$$ *Kongens Nytorv 17.* (p 94)

Best for Courtyard Dining
★★ Restaurant Zeleste $$$$ *Store Strandstræde 6.* (p 99)

Best Place to People Watch
★★ Café Europa $$ *Amagertorv 1.* (p 93)

Best Sea Views
★★★ Marienlyst Restaurant $$$$ *Nordre Strandvej 2, Helsingør.* (p 102)

Best Ice Cream
★★ Vaffelbageren $ *Nyhavn 49.* (p 102)

Most Fashion-conscious Hotel Restaurant
★★ Bleu $$$$ *Hotel Sankt Petri, Krystalgade 22.* (p 133)

Best American Diner
★ FRONT Diner $$ *Hotel FRONT, Sankt Annæ Plads 21.* (p 97)

Best View from an Open-air Café
★★ Sommerhuset $$ *Churchilparken 7A.* (p 101)

Most Romantic Restaurant
★★★ Sankt Gertruds Kloster $$$$ *Hauser Plads 32.* (p 100)

Best Gourmet Destination
★★★ Nimb $$$$ *Bernstorffsgade 5.* (p 80)

Most Laid-back Eatery
★ Bang & Jensen $$ *Istedgade 130.* (p 93)

Best for Hungry Kids
★ Hard Rock Café $$ *Vesterbrogade 3.* (p 98)

Lunchtime at Bang & Jensen.

★ **kids** **Bang & Jensen** VESTER-BRO *BRUNCH* Boho and laid-back, this is *the* Vesterbro hotspot for a lazy Sunday brunch. Sit on the street and catch the sun or relax with a paper in the slightly scruffy backroom over all-day breakfasts, enormous salads and pasta dishes. *Istedgade 130* ☎ *+45 3325 5318. www.bangogjensen.dk. Entrees 55DKK–75DKK. MC, V. Lunch & dinner daily. Bus 2A, 5A, 216. Map p 90.*

★★★ **Bo Bech at Restaurant Paustian** ØSTERBRO *INTERNA-TIONAL* Danish chef, Bo Bech, leads the way in molecular cooking. Splash out on his daily changing 'Alchemist' menu, served in a smart restaurant within Denmark's smartest design showrooms. Sample bread infused with liquorice, langoustines smoked in spruce needles, and pigeon cooked with beetroot. A big treat at a big price! *Kalkbrænderiløbskaj 2.* ☎ *+45 3918 5501. www.restaurantpaustian.dk. Four set menus from lunch at 300DKK to dinner at 750DKK. AE, DC, MC, V. Lunch Dinner Mon–Sat. Train: S-Tog to Nordhavn. Map p 90.*

★★ **Brasserie Petri** LATIN QUAR-TER *ASIAN FUSION* Found in the impossibly hip lobby of the Hotel Sankt Petri. There's a concise menu of Asian fusion dishes (sashimi, tuna tartare, beef with fava bean salad) and a well-chosen wine list. *Krystal-gade 22.* ☎ *+45 3345 9100. www. hotelsktpetri.com. Entrees 225DKK–245DKK. AE, DC, MC, V. Lunch & dinner daily. Metro: Nørreport. Map p 90.*

★★ **Café Europa** STRØGET *PATIS-SERIE* Sip an award-winning espresso in stylish surroundings on the corner of Læderstræde and Amagertorv, the very heart of Copenhagen's pedestrianized shop-ping streets. You are in pole position to watch Copenhagen passing by while indulging in strawberry cheesecake or a carrot-and-orange gateau. *Amagertorv 1.* ☎ *+45 3314 2889. Entrees 135DKK–200DKK. AE, MC, V. Breakfast, lunch & dinner daily; Thur–Sat until 1am. Metro: Kongens Nytorv. Map p 90.*

★★ **Café Glyptotek** RÅDHUS-PLADSEN *DANISH* Hidden away in the palm-and-statue filled Winter

Café Glyptotek.

Garden at the NY Carlsberg Glyptotek (see p 14), this smart compact café is the perfect pitstop for organic teas, Florentines, and patisserie following an afternoon exploring the sculpture galleries. Gourmet open sandwiches of prawns, herring or pork are served at lunchtime. *Dantes Plads 7.* ☎ *+45 3341 8128. www.metteblomsterberg. dk. Entrees 50DKK–250DKK. MC, V. Lunch Tue–Sun. Bus 2A, 5A, 151. Map p 90.*

Café Ketchup TIVOLI *FUSION* You'll not find a ketchup bottle in sight in Tivoli's oldest restaurant, established in 1843. Instead there's a plush mirror-topped bar, crisp white linen, glass ceilings, and a large terrace overlooking Tivoli's open-air stage (see p 120). The short menu is a delicate fusion of Danish, French, and Asian cuisine; try smoked swordfish with wasabi or Danish fillet of beef. They do a cracking Sunday brunch (scrambled eggs, salmon, pancakes) as well. *Vesterbrogade 3.* ☎ *+45 3375 0755. Entrees 200DKK–225DKK. AE, DC, MC, V. Lunch & dinner Sun–Thur daily. Bus 2A, 5A, 151. Map p 90.*

★ **Café Oscar** FREDERIKSSTADEN *CAFÉ SNACKS* An intimate Bredgade venue for mid-morning hot chocolate and pastries, usually resonating to the chatter of smart ladies carrying bulging shopping bags. Burgers, fish cutlets and heaped salads are available all afternoon, along with organic juices, coffees, and wines. *Bredgade 58.* ☎ *+45 3312 5010. www.cafeoscar.dk. Entrees 95DKK–120DKK. MC, V. Lunch daily (open until10pm Mon–Sat, 9pm Sun, kitchen closes at 5pm). Metro: Kongens Nytorv. Map p 90.*

★★★ **Café Petersborg** FRED-ERIKSSTADEN *SMØRREBRØD* Open for business since 1746, **Café Petersborg** was a once favorite with Russian naval officers. The place

Cap Horn was the first organic restaurant along Nyhavn.

is full of rickety charm and equally charming waiting staff. Order schnitzel or tender steak for mains but don't miss out on the best herring in town, served marinated, pickled and curried. *Bredgade 76.* ☎ *+45 3312 5016. www.cafe-petersborg.dk. Entrees 50DKK–140DKK. MC, V. Lunch and dinner Mon–Fri; lunch Sat. Metro: Kongens Nytorv. Map p 90.*

★★ **Café à Porta** KONGENS NYTORV *DANISH* Radiating faded Belle Epoque glamour, **Café à Porta** sits on Copenhagen's massive central square and you'll pay for the privilege of eating under the city's most ornate ceiling. At least you're in good company as you tuck into vast sandwiches stuffed with prime beef or crispy seafood salad. Storyteller Hans Christian Andersen regularly popped into the café—then known as Mini's—when he lived next door. *Kongens Nytorv 17.* ☎ *+45 3311 0500. www.cafeaporta. dk. Entrees 185DKK–235DKK. MC, V.*

Lunch & dinner Mon–Sat. Metro: Kongens Nytorv. Map p 90.

★ **Café René** TIVOLI *BRASSERIE*
A well-priced option only a step away from Tivoli (see p 10). Inside it resembles a French brasserie, with a brass-topped bar and a menu of burgers, grills, and a wide choice of fish dishes. Try *Stjerneskud*—fried and boiled plaice with prawns and caviar—it certainly chased away my lunchtime hunger pangs. *Axel Torv 6. ☎ +45 3314 8501. Entrees 80DKK–180DKK. MC, V. Lunch & dinner daily. Bus: 2A, 5A, 151. Map p 90.*

★ **Café Ultimo** TIVOLI *ITALIAN*
Light-filled Ultimo has the air of a large Victorian conservatory plumped in the middle of Tivoli (see p 10). It can be heaving on some evenings although the cheery staff do a fantastic job of keeping everybody happy. Expect the usual Italian fodder, plates of steaming spaghetti, pizzas, and carafes of red wine. One of Torben Olsen's number of Copenhagen restaurants, this is surprisingly reasonable for its location in Tivoli. *Vesterbrogade 3. ☎ +45 3375 0751. www.cafeultimotivoli.dk. Entrees 100DKK–220DKK. AE, MC, V. Lunch dinner daily. Bus 2A, 5A, 151. Map p 90.*

★ **Café Wilder** CHRISTIANSHAVN *FRENCH/ITALIAN* Popular with the locals, this raucous café in a restored Christianshavn canal house can be chaotic in the evenings with cramped tables, loud conversation and flowing beer. During the less frenzied daytime, drop by for a lunch of fresh tomatoes and mozzarella on homemade ciabatta or an early evening glass of wine huddled under the extraordinary painting of a nude Anita Ekberg. *Wildersgade 56. ☎ +45 3254 7183. www.cafe wilder.dk. Entrees 70DKK–145DKK. MC, V. Lunch & dinner daily. Metro: Christianshavn Torv. Map p 90.*

★★ **Café Zirup** STRÆDET *INTERNATIONAL* Located on a street packed with buzzing bars and restaurants, Zirup is always packed with gorgeous and trendy students tucking into plates of nachos or Thai beef salad or hogging the massive bar sipping daiquiris and downing pints of lager. On cool evenings the overspill huddles together under blankets and heaters outside. *Læderstræde 32. ☎ +45 3313 5060. www.zirup.dk. Entrees 129DKK–169DKK. MC, V. Lunch Mon–Thur; lunch & dinner Fri–Sat. Metro: Nørreport. Map p 90.*

Café Ultimo.

The elegant dining room at Herman.

★★ Cap Horn NYHAVN *SEAFOOD*
Housed in a 17th-century townhouse overlooking the canal, Cap Horn was an early leader of Copenhagen's organic revolution. Try the superb fresh langoustines and wild duck dressed with apple chutney and blueberries. It's always crowded inside so grab a table under the awnings outside and tuck in! *Nyhavn 21.* ☎ *+45 3312 8504. www.caphorn.dk. Entrees 130DKK–200DKK. AE, MC, V. Lunch &*

Ebisu at Custom House.

dinner daily. Metro: Kongens Nytorv. Map p 90.

★★★ Custom House NYHAVN
ITALIAN/JAPANESE/GRILL   Sir Terence Conran's gastronomic emporium is housed in an ex-customs house overlooking the Øresund. Along with two sleek bars, bright white Bacino offers a classy Italian menu, Ebisu specializes in obscenely expensive (even by Copenhagen standards) Japanese cuisine, while the better-value Bar and Grill produces roasts, steaks, and burgers. Round off your night with a cocktail in the bar and watch the boats pass by. *Havnegade 44.* ☎ *+45 3331 0130. www.custom house.dk. Entrees 155DKK–295DKK. Set menu in Ebisu up to 795DKK for two. AE, DC, MC, V. Lunch & dinner daily. Metro: Kongens Nytorv. Map p 90).*

★★★ Era Ora CHRISTIANSHAVN
ITALIAN   Under the watchful eye of Fabio Donadoni, Era Ora is the only Michelin-starred Italian restaurant in Denmark. Deservedly so; the décor is elegant, the terrace overlooks Christianshavn Kanal, and the waiters are

charming. The wine list features a range of enticing Italian wines and the light Italian dishes, such as *ferretti* pasta with mushrooms and veal tenderloin, are simply superb. *Reservations required*. Donadoni has two other venues under his belt that are worth checking out: Tuscan home cooking at **L'Altro** (Torvegade 62, ☎ +45 3254 5406) and the canteen-style fish restaurant **Acquamarina**. *Borgergade 17A,* ☎ *+45 3311 1721. Overgaden Neden Vandet 33B.* ☎ *+45 3254 0693. www.era-ora.dk. Four courses 680DKK; five courses 780DKK. AE, DC, MC, V. Lunch & dinner Mon–Sat. Metro: Christianshavn. Map p 90.*

★ kids **FRONT Diner** NYHAVN *AMERICAN DINER* Huge portions and the laid-back atmosphere of this hotel diner makes it worth a visit. Tables may be cramped and the service can be patchy but it always comes with a smile—and the portions are vast. The casual vibe is well suited to reluctant teenagers, who will squeeze out a smile for the burgers and huge vats of spicy chili. Caesar salads and chicken melts much in demand, followed by cheesecake and all-American apple pie. *Hotel FRONT, Sankt Annæ Plads*

Tuscan home cooking at L'Altro.

21. ☎ *+45 3313 3400. www.front.dk. Entrees 100DKK–220DKK. AE, MC, V. Lunch & dinner daily. Metro: Kongens Nytorv. Map p 90.*

★★★ Green **Geranium** FREDERIKSSTADEN *GOURMET ORGANIC* Owned by current culinary darlings, Rasmus Kofoed and Søren Ledet, and already the possessor of one Michelin star, Geranium was rightly voted Copenhagen's Restaurant of the Year in 2008. The mainly organic menu features the finest crab, lemon sole, or tender venison. In summer the terrace overlooking Kongens Have (see p 86) is great for post-prandial coffees. *Kronprinsessegade 13.* ☎ *+45 3066 8882. www.kongenshave.com. Entrees 250DKK–355DKK. AE, DC, MC, V. Lunch & dinner Tue–Fri; dinner Sat. Metro: Kongens Nytorv. Map p 90.*

★ kids **Hard Rock Café** TIVOLI *BURGER BAR* The perfect antidote for over-excited kids who have run themselves ragged in Tivoli. Service is brisk and courteous, the burgers and steaks are just what you would expect from this international chain, and the sensible prices make this a sure hit with families. *Vesterbrogade 3.* ☎ *+45 3312 4333. www.hardrock.*

com. *Entrees 100DKK–180DKK. AE, DC, MC, V. Lunch & dinner daily. Bus 2A, 5A, 151. Map p 90.*

★★★ **Herman** TIVOLI *GOURMET* Denmark's latest top chef Thomas Herman brought a new gourmet palace to the Copenhagen gastronomic scene when he opened in May 2008. Time will tell whether he will receive a coveted Michelin star during the next couple of years for his ever-changing haute-cuisine menu but the signs are looking positive and it's well worth deciding for yourself. Surprisingly plain dining room. *Hotel Nimb, Bernstorffsgade 5.* ☎ *+45 8870 0000. www.nimb.dk. Four courses: 695DKK; six courses 850DKK. AE, DC, MC, V. Lunch & dinner Mon–Fri; dinner Sat. Bus 2A, 5A, 151. Map p 90.*

★★★ **Lê Lê** VESTERBRO *VIETNAMESE* You can't book tables for Copenhagen's hottest restaurant in trendy Vesterbro, so join the queues at the cavernous bar, all happily anticipating top-notch Vietnamese fusion food. Savor the dim sum starters, followed by delicate pancakes stuffed with chili chicken,

The traditional interior of Leonore Christine.

sweet and sour pork or delicious rice noodles flavored with coriander and lemon grass. The atmosphere is chaotic but the service is friendly despite the warehouse-size proportions of the venue. *Vesterbrogade 40.* ☎ *+45 3331 3125. Entrees 155DKK–200DKK. MC, V. Dinner Mon, Wed–Sun. Bus 2A, 5A, 216. Map p 90.*

Oasi d'Italia—a hit with families.

★★★ Leonore Christine NYHAVN SEAFOOD Copenhagen's oldest building has been standing since 1681; this charming Nyhavn restaurant has gently sloping floors and the walls are dotted with portraits of Danish kings and queens. In the evening candlelight, it's a very romantic spot. Lunchtime best buys include pickled herrings served with capers and a rich pork pâté smothered with bacon and mushrooms. *Nyhavn 9. ☎ +45 3313 5040. www .leonore-christine.dk. Entrees 190DKK–240DKK. AE, DC, MC, V. Lunch & dinner daily. Metro: Kongens Nytorv. Map p 90.*

★★★ kids Peder Oxe LATIN QUARTER DANISH Book in advance for a blowout dinner at one of Copenhagen's oldest and certainly noisiest restaurants, with arguably the most beautiful waiting staff in Copenhagen. You'll find a series of lively dining rooms with wooden floors and tables squeezed in at odd angles. Dishes range from organic steak to melt-in-the-mouth sole and diners stock up with fresh salads at the buffet. Set it off with Chablis and round off with a selection of tasty Danish cheeses. *Gråbrødretorv 11. ☎ +45 3311 0077. www.pederoxe.dk. Entrees 125DKK–200DKK. AE, DC, MC, V. Lunch & dinner daily. Metro: Kongens Nytorv. Map p 90.*

★ kids Restaurant Bali KONGENS NYTORV INDONESIAN Decorated with Indonesian flair and crammed with tiny tables amid a riot of Balinese artifacts, weekends see this fun place packed out with celebrating Danes. Go for the *rijstaffel*, a spicy selection of rices, curries, satays, pickles, and salads all served at once and kept warm on

Decorations at restaurant Bali.

heaters at your table. Add chili-laden *sambal* sauce if you need a bit more bite. *Kongens Nytorv 19. ☎ +45 3311 0808. www3.aok. dk/infosites/3276/3.html. Rijstaffel 295DKK for two people. DC, MC, V. Open: daily 12pm–12am. Metro: Kongens Nytorv. Map p 90.*

Restaurant Els NYHAVN DANISH GOURMET This atmospheric candle-lit dining room with Art Nouveau murals of dancing girls on the walls is reputedly one of the finest restaurants in Copenhagen. On the night I visited, the food was variable (starters of carpaccio of beef and smoked swordfish were excellent) and the service disintegrated as the night wore on. Maybe it was an off night so let's give it the benefit of the doubt. *Store Strandstræde 3. ☎ +45 3314 1341. www.restaurant-els.dk. Entrees 185DKK–285DKK. AE, DC, MC, V. Dinner Mon–Sat. Metro: Kongens Nytorv. Map p 90.*

★★ kids Restaurant Oasi d'Italia STRÆDET ITALIAN Always busy in the evening with Danish families. And no wonder; they love the informal atmosphere, and reasonably priced choice of pasta and oven-baked pizza dishes as well as the excellent tiramisù. A bargain by Copenhagen standards. *Kompagnistræde 19. ☎ +45 3311 1119. Entrees 60DKK–190DKK. MC, V. Lunch & dinner daily. Metro: Kongens Nytorv. Map p 90.*

Restaurant Zeleste NYHAVN DANISH/FRENCH With a vine-strewn courtyard at the back ,and a bow-fronted dining room inside, Zeleste deserves the prize for the most visually appealing restaurant in town. Luckily the standard of food matches the décor; Danish dishes with French overtones include

The Royal Cafe.

grilled lobster and venison cooked in blueberries and wine, with French cheeses to follow. Seasonal specials change nightly. *Store Strandstræde 6.* ☎ *+45 3316 0606. www.zeleste.dk. Entrees 125DKK–225DKK. AE, DC, MC, V. Lunch & dinner Mon–Sat. Metro: Kongens Nytorv. Map p 90.*

★★★ **The Royal Café** STRØGET *SMUSHI* This café gives a new meaning to the word 'kitsch'. Think pink walls, a metallic sheen on the glitzy leaf-patterned ceiling and spoof Old Masters on the walls. There's an array of coffees and teas and the lunchtime menu includes 'smushi', a happy combination of smørrebrød and sushi—curried herring, burgers and tasty fish fillets all served in miniature. Other options include soups, salads, and tangy lemon desserts. *Amagertorv 6.* ☎ *+45 3814 9527. www.theroyalcafe. dk. Entrees 45DKK–120DKK. AE, MC, V. Lunch daily. Metro: Kongens Nytorv. Map p 90.*

★★ **SALT** NYHAVN *DANISH MODERN EUROPEAN* The nautical theme of the Admiral Hotel (see p 127) continues in the dining room, where Chef Rasmus Møller Nielsen is garnering applause for his confident European-style dishes with a

Danish twist. The menu changes seasonally and might feature poached crab served with mushrooms and spinach or oxtail and sweetbreads. There's a direct shuttle from here to the Operaen (see p 119) across the Øresund. *Toldbodgade 24.* ☎ *+45 3374 1414. www.admiralhotel.dk. Entrees 195DKK–275DKK. AE, DC, MC, V. Lunch & dinner daily. Metro: Kongens Nytorv. Map p 90.*

★★★ **Sankt Gertruds Kloster** NØRREPORT *INTERNATIONAL/ BRASSERIE* The restaurant occupies several floors of a medieval convent; most atmospheric is the basement wine vault flickering in candlelight, which comes into its own at party time, when the tables fill with celebrating locals. There are several different menus to choose from as well as à la carte; foie gras and artichoke soup are popular starters, while Entrees range from sea bass to goose stuffed with mushrooms, accompanied by a thoughtful wine list. *Hauser Plads 32.* ☎ *+45 3314 6630. www.sankt gertrudskloster.dk. Entrees: 188DKK– 378DKK; three-course dinner and wine 618DKK. AE, DC, MC, V. Dinner daily. Metro: Nørreport. Map p 90.*

★★★ **SARS Kommandøren** NYHAVN *SEAFOOD* One of my favorite places on Nyhavn to stop for a leisurely lunch of marinated herring and *smørrebrød,* piled high with salmon, garlicky mayo, and dill. On sunny days, grab a table under the awning by the street-side bar and order a chilled dark lager. Inside, the cheery dining room has the bare bricks walls and uneven floors of a typical 17th-century Nyhavn canal house. *Nyhavn 15.* ☎ *+45 3314 5614. www.sars.dk. Entrees 189DKK–229DKK. AE, MC, V. Dinner daily. Metro: Kongens Nytorv. Map p 90.*

★★ kids **Sommerhuset** FRED-ERIKSSTADEN *DANISH* With views over the Kastellet (see p 16) and the extravagant Gefion Fountain, this bustling little café is the place to sip a glass of champagne and sit back in the sun. Sample the all-day breakfast (Parma ham, cheese, herrings, pastries, yogurts and smoothies on offer). The open space and ice cream stand attract families. Combine brunch here with a visit to the adjacent Resistance Museum (see p 58). *Churchilparken 7A.* ☎ +45 3332 1314. www.cafesommerhuset. dk. Entrees 88DKK–125DKK. MC, V. *Dinner daily 9am–12am. Closed Nov–Apr. Metro: Kongens Nytorv. Map p 90.*

★★★ **Søren K** CHRISTIANSHAVN *MODERN EUROPEAN* Named after Copenhagen's most mournful philosopher, Søren Kierkegaard, this is an expensive night out but worth the price for the views over the Øresund from the first floor of the Royal Library's *Sorte Diamond* (Back Diamond, see p 30) and the sleek gray minimalist décor. Its light modern European fare is of the highest standard, introducing flashes of nouvelle cuisine cooked under the auspices of restaurant head Gustav Vilholm. The menu boasts lots of vegetarian options, unusual in many Danish restaurants, healthy grilled fish options, and thinly sliced carpaccio. In summer sit outside on the terrace overlooking the sea. *Søren Kierkegaards Plads 1.* ☎ +45 3347 4949. www.soerenk.dk. Tasting menu 500DKK. Lunch & dinner Mon–Sat. DC, MC, V. Metro: Kongens Nytorv. Map p 90.*

★★★ **Spicylicious** VESTERBRO *THAI* An elegant and romantic Thai restaurant in Vesterbro; orchids hang in the windows and Thai paintings give the room a splash of color. There is a small chill-out area for pre-dinner drinks while you wait for a table. The food here is tasty and good value with Thai favorites such as spiced chicken satay, king prawns dipped in coconut and beef with pad Thai noodles. *Istedgade 27.* ☎ +45 3322 8533. www.restaurant spicylicious.dk. Entrees 95DKK–150DKK. DC, MC, V. Dinner daily 5pm–11pm. Bus 2A, 5A, 216. Map p 90.*

SALT at the Admiral Hotel.

★★ Vaffelbageren

NYAHVN *ICE CREAM* The best ice cream in central Copenhagen, where homemade cones are piled with toffee, coffee, or strawberry flavors, plus several kinds of icy slush from a gurgling machine by the doorway. Eat in or sit on the decking outside the new Kongelige Teater Skuespilhuset (Danish Royal Playhouse, see p 122) and watch the world go by. *Nyhavn 49.* ☎ *+45 3314 0698. Lunch & dinner daily. Metro: Kongens Nytorv. Map p 90.*

Homemade waffle cones.

www.peccatidigola.dk. Entrees 100DKK– 220DKK. AE, DC, MC, V. Dinner daily 5pm–10pm. Train: Helsingør. Map p 90.

Hillerød

★★ kids Spisestedet Leonora HILLERØD *DANISH SNACKS* Tucked in the shadows of fairy-tale Frederiksborg Slot (see p 52), this buzzing café has airy dining rooms and a large cobbled terrace overlooking meadows. Plates of fish fillets, roast meats and pickles, salads, and open sandwiches are guaranteed to buck up feet weary from traipsing around the castle. *Frederiksborg Slot, Hillerød.* ☎ *+45 4826 7516. www. leonora.dk. Entrees 60DKK–110DKK. MC, V. Lunch daily. Train: Hillerød. Map p 90.*

Helsingør

★★★ Marienlyst Restaurant

HELSINGØR *INTERNATIONAL* An exceptional hotel restaurant with a regularly changing menu featuring lobster, prawns, grilled meat and steak dishes plus a vegetarian option. If you're here on a clear evening, grab a table facing the Øresund to watch the sun slip down into the sea. *Hotel Marienlyst, Nordre Strandvej 2, Helsingør.* ☎ *+45 4921 4000. www.marienlyst.dk. Two courses: 285DKK; five courses: 485DKK. AE, DC, MC, V. Dinner daily. Train: Helsingør. Map p 90.*

★★ Peccati di Gola HELSINGØR

ITALIAN In an ancient townhouse on the edge of Helsingør's old town, this Sardinian-run restaurant offers well-presented dishes in cozy half-timbered surroundings. Opt for antipasti of mussels followed by spaghetti with scampi and pesto. There is decking outside for eating *al fresco* on balmy nights. *Kongensgade 6, Helsingør.* ☎ *+45 4929 8283.*

Malmö

★★ kids Mai Thai MALMÖ, SWEDEN *THAI* Join local office workers on this rickety boat in Malmö's booming docklands for a spicy lunch of Thai pad noodles flavored with lime or shellfish with red curry. There's also a sundeck for eating outside if the weather permits. Nothing fancy, just simple, wholesome food, and preferable to paying over the odds in Gamla Stan, Malmö's touristy old town (see p 150). *Docktorget 1, Malmö.* ☎ *+11 40 78810. Entrees 100DKK–140DKK. MC, V. Open: Lunch–dinner Mon–Thur; lunch Fri; dinner Sat–Sun. Train: Malmö. Map p 90.* ●

The Best Nightlife

Copenhagen Nightlife

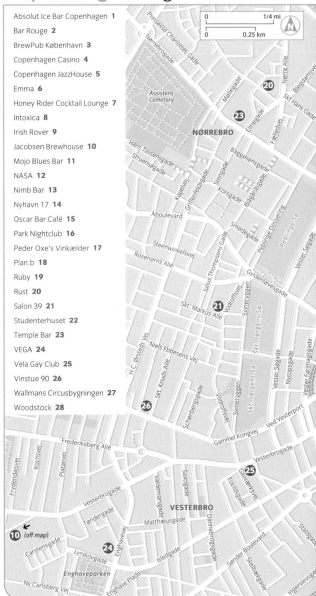

(off map) ↗ 16

ØSTERBRO

Blegdamsvej
Fredensgade
Ryesgade
Ryesgade
Sortedam Dossering
Øster Søgade
Sortedams Sø
Øster Søgade
Sølvgade
Ole Suhrs Gade
Øster Farimagsgade
Stockholmsgade

Garnisons Cemetery
Visbygade
Oslo Plads
Østbanegade
Folke Bernadottes Allé

Holmens Cemetery
Upsalagade

Østre Anlæg
Denmark's National Gallery

Delfingade
Gernersgade
Grønningen

Copenhagen University
Øster Farimagsgade
Solvgade

Copenhagen University
Sølvgade

Skt Pauls Gade
Fredericiagade
Klerkegade
Adelgade
Borgergade
Store Kongensgade
Bredgade

Botanisk Have
Gothersgade

18
Frederiksborggade
ndersgade

Rosenborg Castle
King's Gardens
Gothersgade

Skt. Annæ Plads

Israels Plads

Landemærket
Frederiksborggade
Nørregade
Fiolstræde

12
Kongens Nytorv

14
Nyhavn
Herluf

Ørsteds Parken
Nørre Voldgade

2
Købmagergade

22
Klareboderne
Kronprinsensgade
Antonigade
Østergade

The Royal Theatre

THE LATIN QUARTER
University

17
9
CITY
5
Amagertorv
Strøget
Østergade
6
Niels Juels Gade

8
Studiestræde

28
Vestergade
Skindergade
Rådhusstræde
Domhuset
11
19
Læderstræde
Højbro Plads
Dybensgade

Holmens Kanal

3
15
City Hall Square
Kompagnistræde
1
7
Stormgade
Frederiksholms Kanal
National Museum

Christiansborg
Tøjhusgade
Slotholmsgade
Børsen

National banken

3
entral ation

City Hall

Dansk Design Centre
H.C. Andersens

Jewish Museum
The Royal Library

Knippelsbro

Strandgade
Havnegade
Wildersgade

Tivoli

Tivoli Concert Hall
Tietgensgade
Glyptoteket
Vester Voldgade
H.C. Andersens Boulevard
Christians Brygge

The Black Diamond

CHRISTIANSHAVN

Torvegade

Bernstorffsgade
Langebro
Langebrogade

Kalvebod Bastion
Enhjørningens Bastion
Panterens Bastion
Stadsgraven

Kalvebod Brygge
Islands Brygge
Thorshavnsgade
Njalsgade
Klaksvigsgade
Amager Boulevard
Weidekampsgade
Artillerivej

4

ISLANDS BRYGGE

SYDHAVNEN
Havne Parken

Nightlife Best Bets

Tuborg and Carlsberg are Copenhagen beers of choice.

Coldest Bar in Town
★★★ Absolut Ice Bar, *Løn-gangstræde 27 (p 108)*

Most Elusive Bar
★★★ Ruby, *Nybrogade 10 (p 110)*

Best for *hygge* (Danish Hospitality)
★★ Nyhavn 17, *Nyhavn 17 (p 107)*

Best for Las Vegas-Style
★★★ Wallmans Circusbygningen, *Jernbanegade 8 (p 112)*

Most Generous Hosts
★★ Irish Rover, *Vimmelskaftet 46 (p 107)*

Weirdest Cocktail Mix
★★ Honey Rider Cocktail Lounge, *Løngangstræde 27 (p 109)*

Best for Celeb-Spotting
★★★ Emma, *Lille Kongensgade 16 (p 110)*

Cheapest Pint
★ Studenterhuset, *Købmagergade 52 (p 108)*

Most Obscure Beers
★★★ Plan.b, *Frederiksborggade 48 (p 108)*

Best for Alternative Music
★★ Rust, *Guldbergsgade 8 (p 112)*

Best for Disco Dancing
★★★ Park Nightclub, *Østerbrogade 79 (p 110)*

Biggest Dance Club
★★★ VEGA, *Enghavevej 40 (p 110)*

Copenhagen Nightlife A to Z

Bars & Pubs

★★★ BrewPub København

RÅDHUSPLADSEN Firmly on the tourist track, this heaving micro-brewery has a changing menu of seven house beers daily, as well as European guest ales. Grab a table in the courtyard to sample the Belgian beer Eté or VesterWeisse wheat beer over traditional English steak pie. *Vestergade 29.* ☎ *+45 3332 0060. www.brewpub.dk. Bus 2A, 5A, 151. Map p 104.*

★★ Irish Rover STRØGET A cav-

ernous Irish pub with big screens showing sport and live folk music every evening. Ma Farrelly's kitchen serves predictable pub grub and the friendly staff have a propensity to hand out free shots! *Vimmelskaftet 46.* ☎ *+45 3333 7393. www.theirish rover.dk. Metro: Kongens Nytorv. Map p 104.*

★ Jacobsen Brewhouse VALBY

Pay a visit to the Carlsberg Brewery (see p 50) and claim your two pints of Tuborg, Carlsberg, or Jacobsen lager (included in the entrance price). This stylish venue with a curved copper bar made from old brewing

The curved copper bar at Jacobsen Brewhouse.

vats serves a selection of rare brews that can only be bought here. *Gamle Carlsberg Vej 11.* ☎ *+45 3327 1314. www.visitcarlsberg.com. Train: Eng-have. Map p 104.*

★★ Nyhavn 17 NYHAVN With

a serious list of whiskies and an

BrewPub København.

Absolut Ice Bar Copenhagen.

endless selection of draught beers (Trappist, stout, dark lagers), this pub has stuck to its nautical Nyhavn roots. Inside is cluttered with old boat propellers and merry crowds spill out onto the street for a convivial late-night atmosphere. Live music is on most nights. *Nyhavn 17.* ☎ *+45 3312 5419. Metro: Kongens Nytorv. Map p 104.*

★★ **Peder Oxe's Vinkælder** LATIN QUARTER   Underneath Peder Oxe restaurant (see p 99), spilling out onto a cobbled medieval square in summer, this is a perfect bar for balmy evenings. Inside these old monastery cellars, space is tight and things can get noisy as the evening unwinds. *Gråbrødretorv 11.* ☎ *+45 3311 0077. www.pederoxe.dk/. Metro: Kongens Nytorv. Map p 104.*

★★★ **Plan.b** NØRREBRO   A bit off the radar but worth the trip for local microbrewed beers and a feeling that you are sitting in an aged aunt's front room. With nearly 500 beers

(bottled and draft) and a selection of wines to choose from, the owner happily dispenses his expertise. *Frederiksborggade 48.* ☎ *+45 3336 3656. www.cafeplanb.dk. Metro: Nørreport. Map p 104.*

★ **Studenterhuset** LATIN QUARTER   Just the place for rubbing shoulders with the next generation of Jacobsens and Kierkegaards. Situated opposite the university halls of residence, this venue is as cheap and homely as you would expect from a student dive. There are party nights with DJs playing hip-hop and techno, as well as Sunday Swing, afternoon jazz and blues sessions. *Købmagergade 52.* ☎ *+45 3532 3861. studenterhuset.com. Metro: Nørreport. Map p 104.*

★★ **Temple Bar** NØRREBRO   A relaxed atmosphere and sagging sofas attracts a young clientele for an early evening beer or cocktail, a chat, and a round of table soccer. There's an entertaining weekly open stage on Tuesday at 9pm for up-and-coming songwriters and performers—be it jugglers or acrobats. *Nørrebrogade 48* ☎ *+45 3537 4414. Metro: Nørreport. Map p 104.*

★★ **Vinstue 90** VESTERBRO   Don't be in a hurry when you visit this traditional Vesterbro bodega, home of 'slow' beer. Here, pouring uncarbonated Carlsberg takes up to 15 minutes per pint; the result is a smooth drink with a wobbly frothy head that stays until the glass is empty. *Gammel Kongevej 90.* ☎ *+45 3331 8490. www.vinstue90.dk. Bus 2A, 5A, 216. Map p 104.*

Designer Bars

★★★ **Absolut Ice Bar Copenhagen** RÅDHUSPLADSEN   Part of a pan-European franchise, the Ice Bar is kept at -5 degrees; sessions for groups of up to 50 last 45 minutes. It is breathtakingly cold but quite

Where to Go

To pick up on the hippest bars and coolest DJs in this fashion-conscious city, look for **Copenhagen This Week**, a monthly English-language listings magazine that gives day-by-day details of what's in and what's not; source it online at www.ctw.dk. Gay and lesbian visitors can check www.out-and-about.dk and ziraf.dk respectively for forthcoming events. Visit Copenhagen Tourist Office can also provide up-to-date information: Gammel Kongevej 1. ☎ +45 3325 7400. www.visitcopenhagen.com.

beautiful to look at. Everything from the walls to the bar and the shots glasses are made of crystal-clear ice; knock back mango-flavored vodka before the glass melts onto your lips. *Løngangstræde 27.* ☎ *+45 7027 5627. www.hotel27.dk. Bus 2A, 5A, 151. Map p 104.*

★ **Bar Rouge** LATIN QUARTER During the week, this ultra-cool bar

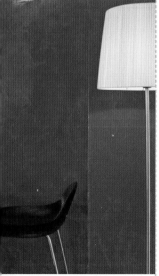

Stylish Bar Rouge, the city's hottest cocktail bar.

serves coffees and goblets of Chablis to well-heeled ladies. At the weekend the music steps up a gear generating the hottest address in town. DJs play ambient music whilst an affluent crowd of thirty-some-things knock back expensive cock-tails. *Krystalgade 22.* ☎ *+45 3345 9100. www.hotelsktpetri.com. Metro: Nørreport. Map p 104.*

★★ **Honey Rider Cocktail Lounge** RÅDHUSPLADSEN A buzzing bar furnished with simple Danish designs in trendy Hotel Twentyseven (see p 133). The 'mixol-ogists' take their job very seriously here, creating cocktails with inge-nious names like the Lip-gloss Mar-tini. It's best at the weekend, when the young-ish hotel clientele mixes effortlessly with on-trend locals. *Løngangstræde 27.* ☎ *+45 7027 5627. www.hotel27.dk. Bus 2A, 5A, 151. Map p 104.*

★★ **Intoxica** RÅDHUSPLADSEN The Polynesian Tiki bar on the ground floor of Hotel Fox (see p 131) is a meeting place for Copenhagen's beautiful party people. Colorful fruity cocktails are stuffed with umbrellas and can be served up in a receptacle decorated as a plastic skull. *Jarmers Plads 3.* ☎ *+45 3338 7030. www.intoxica.dk. Bus 2A, 5A, 151. Map p 104.*

★★ **Nimb Bar** TIVOLI   Another top-notch hangout in the Nimb empire (see p 132), with a huge fireplace perfect for escaping to on rainy spring afternoons. Take afternoon tea (served with champagne of course) with the Copenhagen moneyed set or sink into a cozy armchair for a digestif after dinner at Herman (see p 98). *Hotel Nimb, Bernstorffsgade 5.* ☎ *+45 8870 0000. www.nimb.dk. Bus 2A, 5A, 151. Map p 104.*

★★★ **Ruby** KONGENS NYTORV   So hip it's almost impossible to find; an elegant cocktail bar in sumptuous rooms hidden behind what looks like a private doorway on the landward side of Nybrogard. Sample the excellent ruby daiquiris, flavored with rhubarb, or go long with an Apple Smash, vodka infused with apple, lime, mint and a kick of champagne. A sophisticated start to any evening. *Nybrogade 10.* ☎ *+45 3395 1203. www.rby.dk. Metro: Kongens Nytorv. Map p 104.*

★★★ **Salon 39** FREDERIKSBERG   In a rapidly gentrifying part of town, this elegant bar with discreet lighting and an unusual cocktail list has caught on fast. There's a short supper menu and occasional jazz too. *Vodroffsvej 39.* ☎ *+45 3920 8039. www.salon39.dk. Metro: Forum. Map p 104.*

Casino

★ **Copenhagen Casino** AMAGER   Try your luck at poker, black jack, punto banco, and roulette at this casino, part of the Radisson SAS Scandinavia complex (see p 29). Dress codes apply and don't forget photo ID even if you're just playing the slots. *Amager Boulevard 70.* ☎ *+45 3396 5965. uk.casino copenhagen.dk. Admission 85DKK. Metro: Amagerbro; Train: Islands Brygge; Bus: 5a, 33. Map p 104.*

Dance Clubs

★★★ **Emma** KONGENS NYTORV   Although advertised as Copenhagen's biggest private party, it's quite easy to get in by dressing smart. Once inside you'll find a swish cocktail bar, a restaurant with classy buffet food, and a club that stays open until the early hours at

Spaced out club NASA.

The curvy wooden bar at VEGA.

the weekend, with DJs and bands. *Lille Kongensgade 16.* ☎ *+45 3311 2020. www.emma.dk. Metro: Kongens Nytorv. Map p 104.*

★ **NASA** NØRREBRO Dress up and be dazzled by the *Barbarella*-style space-age whiteness of this club. Even the fish in the aquarium at the entrance are white. Popular with wealthy celebs, who gather here to dance to house and mainstream soul. *Gothersgade 8F.* ☎ *+45 3393 7415. www.nasa.dk. Metro: Nørreport. Map p 104.*

★★★ **Park Nightclub** ØSTERBRO The colorful retro styling of this club and laid-back soundtrack of 70s and 80s pop attracts a young crowd. Expect disco balls and bubble patterns projected on the walls to complete the vibe. *Østerbrogade 79.* ☎ *+45 3525 1661. www.park.dk. Train: Østerport. Map p 104.*

★★ **VEGA** VESTERBRO In the heart of once-gritty Vesterbro, VEGA is in a listed 1950s building, all wooden panels and loudly tiled floors. The mix of concerts and weekend club nights with top guest DJs makes this venue immensely popular; expect to queue to get in. *Enghavevej 40.* ☎ *+45 3325 7011. www.vega.dk. Train: Enghave. Map p 104.*

★★★ **Woodstock** RÅDHUSPLADSEN A nightly medley of dance hits from the 1960s to the 1990s,

Dress Code

Going out in Copenhagen is largely a casual affair; jeans and trainers suffice in most bars, cafés, and pubs. However, if you intend to encroach on clubbing territory, dress to impress to get past the velvet ropes. Designer bars (see p 108) with door policies and cocktail menus also expect a modicum of effort on the sartorial front. In general, clubs get going quite late so aim to get there after midnight. There are plenty of bars and pubs to keep party animals going until then.

Entertainer at Wallmans.

complete with cover bands and DJs spinning the chart hits of Abba, Madonna, and Village People. Thursday is the night for contemporary rock hits and a younger crowd. *Vestergade 12* ☎ *+45 3311 2071. www.woodstock.dk. Bus 2A, 5A, 151. Map p 104.*

Dinner Show

★★ **Wallmans Circusbygningen** TIVOLI   Vegas comes to Copenhagen in a glitzy series of themed dinner shows, with live music, singing, stunts, and acrobatics all thrown in. The circular venue, once a circus ring, has four dance floors for an after-dinner boogie. *Jernbanegade 8.* ☎ *+45 3316 3700. www.wallmans.dk. Tickets 575DKK–845DKK includes dinner. Bus 2A, 5A, 15. Map p 104.*

Gay Copenhagen

★★ **Oscar Bar Café** RÅDHUSPLADSEN   Copenhagen's best-known gay café serves draught beers, coffees and a straightforward menu with noodles and tiger prawns or smoked salmon. Come down at the weekend to the Friday night party, when DJs play R'n'B and soul. *Rådhuspladsen 77.* ☎ *+45 3312 0999.*

www.oscarbarcafe.dk. Bus 2A, 5A, 151. Map p 104.

★ **Vela Gay Club** VESTERBRO Small, cramped lesbian nightclub with a vague Oriental theme. The tiny bar is always packed but the party really gets going after midnight at the weekend, helped along by a cracking cocktail menu. *Viktoriagade 2-4.* ☎ *+45 3331 3419. www.velagay club.dk. Bus 2A, 5A, 151. Map p 104.*

Live Music

★ **Copenhagen JazzHouse** LATIN QUARTER   Jazz concerts every night but Monday, followed by a dance club in the basement that kicks off after midnight. The venue is a little worn at the edges but at the time of writing was undergoing a facelift. Buy tickets through the website—they are heavily discounted. *Niels Hemmingsens Gade 10.* ☎ *+45 3315 2600. www.jazzhouse.dk. Metro: Nørreport. Map p 104.*

★★ **Mojo Blues Bar** RÅDHUS-PLADSEN   Hugely popular blues club with live sessions nightly and walls plastered with black-and-white images of venerable old blues players. Get there before 9.30pm to ensure a seat; book for Friday and Saturday nights, when there is an admission charge. *Løngangstræde 21c.* ☎ *+45 2344 9777. www.mojo. dk. Bus: 2A, 5A, 151. Map p 104.*

★★ **Rust** NØRREBRO   Alternative music fans should check out one of the four club nights or regular gigs held here (the latter consists of mostly indie and hip-hop bands looking for a break. Wednesday club night Heat draws in trendy urbanites dedicated to hip-hop and drum'n'bass. Saturday nights last until 5am with DJs, house, and rock, plus the odd live band. *Guldbergsgade 8.* ☎ *+45 3524 5200. www.rust.dk. Metro: Nørreport. Map p 104.* ●

Copenhagen Arts & Entertainmen

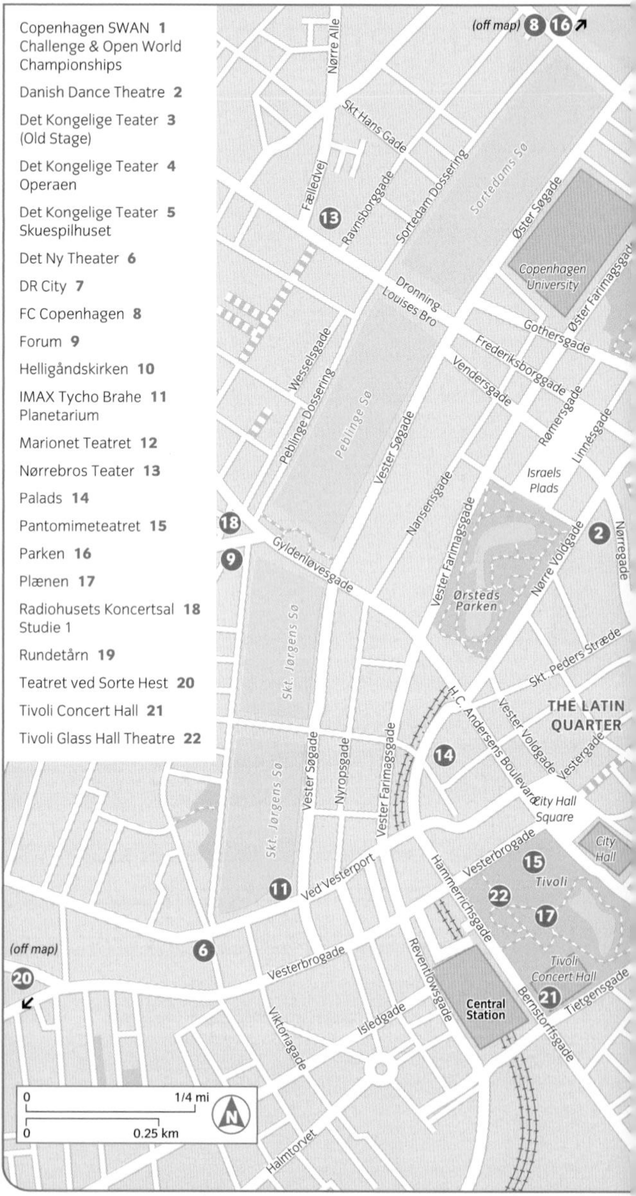

Arts & Entertainment Best Bets

Best Acoustics
★★★ Det Kongelige Teater Operaen, *Ekvipagemestervej 10 (p 119)*

Best Addition to the Arts Scene
★★★ Det Kongelige Teater Skuespilhus, *Sankt Annæ Plads 36 (p 122)*

Biggest Rock Festival
★★★ Roskilde Festival, *Roskilde (p 158)*

Best for Dance Performances
★★★ Danish Dance Theatre, *Nørregade 39 (p 118)*

Best Venue for Musicals
★★ Det Ny Theater, *Gammel Kongevej 29 (p 117)*

Best Venue to see Hamlet
★★★ Kronborg Castle, *Helsingør (p 147)*

Best Live Music Venue
★★ Plænen (Open-air Stage Tivoli), *Vesterbrogade 3 (p 120)*

Biggest Moviehouse
★★ Palads, *Axeltorv 9 (p 119)*

Best Spot for Formal Dressing
★★★ Det Kongelige Teater Old Stage, *Kongens Nytorv 2 (p 122)*

Strangest Venue for Concerts
★★ Rundetårn, *Købmagergade 52a (p 118)*

Harlequin performance at the Pantomimeteatret in Tivoli.

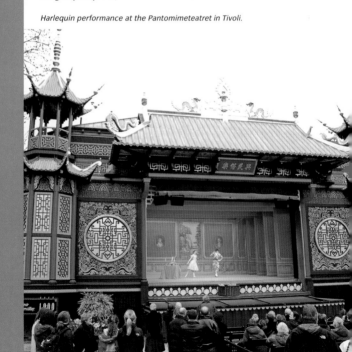

Arts & Entertainment A to Z

Children's' Entertainment

★ **kids Marionet Teatret** KON-GENS HAVE Families can watch up to two free kiddies' shows a day over the summer months at . Subject matter is quite eccentric. You'll find the puppet theater hidden away in the north-east corner of Kongens Have in a small pavilion. *Kronprinsessgade 2. ☎ +45 3542 6472. www.marionetteatret.dk. Tickets free. June 1–Sept 7 2pm and 3pm. Metro: Nørreport. Map p 114.*

★★★ **kids Pantomimeteatret Tivoli** TIVOLI Decked out in the style of a garish Chinese pavilion and located just inside the main Tivoli entrance, this theater features mime, dance, and panto for a young audience. *Vesterbrogade 3. ☎ +45 3312 1012. billetnet.dk. Ticket prices vary. Bus 2A, 5A, 15. Map p 114.*

Concert Halls

★★ **kids Det Ny Theater** VESTERBRO Built in 1908, the majestic Danish home of international musicals is highly ornate, inside and out. *Gammel Kongevej 29. ☎ +45 3325 5075. www.detnyteater.dk. Ticket prices vary. Bus: 2A, 5A, 216. Map p 114.*

★★ **DR City** ØRESTADEN A brand-new venue for concerts opened in January 2009 in the visionary new development of Ørestaden (see p 31). The venue is the creation of French architect Jean Nouvel and boasts an audience capacity of 1,600, a stage that accommodates 200, and four recording studios. *Ørestads Boulevard 19. ☎ +45 3520 8100. www.dr.dk/koncerthuset. Ticket prices vary. Metro: Vestamager. Map p 114.*

★★ **Helligåndskirken** STRØGET Catch weekly organ recitals over the

Det Ny Theater lights up at night.

summer months in this grand old red-brick church. A series of the classics (Brahms, Fauré) and Gregorian chant recitals can be heard here in the winter. *Niels Hemmingsens Gade 5. ☎ +45 7022 2442. www.helligaandskirken.dk. Tickets free–140DKK. Metro: Kongens Nytorv. Map p 114.*

★★ **Nørrebros Teater** NØRRE-BRO Known for encouraging up-and-coming talent, the theater puts on mainstream musicals, dance performances and comedy. The current director is homegrown stand-up Jonotan Spang. *Ravnsborggade 3. ☎ + 45 3520 0900. www.nbt.dk. Ticket prices vary. Metro: Nørreport. Map p 114.*

★★ **Radiohusets Koncertsal Studie 1** FREDERIKSBERG Danish radio's broadcasting center is housed in a Utilitarian-style building with a 1,200-seater concert hall and an organ with 7,000 gilded pipes

Organ recitals and other classic concerts take place at the Helligåndskirken.

dominating the auditorium. It's also home to the Danish National Radio Symphony Orchestra and Radio Choir, both of whom play regular concerts here. *Julius Thomsensgade 1.* ☎ *+45 3520 6262. www.billetnet. dk. Tickets 60DKK–100DKK. Metro: Forum. Map p 114.*

★★ Rundetårn (Round Tower)

LATIN QUARTER   A mixed series of concerts held the year round, from guitar soloists playing Rodrigo to Scarlatti clavichord concerts or samba jazz sessions. They are held in the Library Hall, which also hosts contemporary art exhibitions. *Købmagergade 52a.* ☎ *+45 3373 0373. www.rundetaarn.dk. Tickets 70DKK–150DKK. Metro: Nørreport. Map p 114.*

★★ Tivoli Concert Hall TIVOLI

Tivoli's main concert hall was built in 1956 and is home to the Tivoli Symphony Orchestra. Nightly performances range from the New York Ballet to chamber ensembles to rock legends. *Tivoli Ticket Office, Vesterbrogade 3.* ☎ *+45 3312 1012. billetnet.dk. Ticket prices vary. Bus 2A, 5A, 15. Map p 114.*

★ kids Tivoli Glass Hall Theatre

TIVOLI   Old-fashioned variety shows of sometimes questionable standards but good family fun, housed in a lovely wrought-iron and glass pavilion. *Tivoli Ticket Office, Vesterbrogade 3.* ☎ *+45 3312 1012. www. billetnet.dk. Ticket prices vary. Bus: 2A, 5A, 15. Map p 114.*

Dance
★★★ Danish Dance Theatre

NORREBRO   Denmark's leading contemporary dance venue has gone from strength to strength under the auspices of English dance meister Tim Rushton. He presents a program of wildly imaginative modern dance so even if you are not usually a fan, give this company a chance. *Nørregade 39.* ☎ *+ 45 3312 1845. www.danskdanseteater.dk. Tickets 160DKK. Metro: Nørreport. Map p 114.*

Film
★★★ kids IMAX Tycho Brahe Planetarium VESTERBRO   Ten-

minute ever-changing 3-D films are shown continually just off the foyer

What's On

For the latest concert, theater, cinema and event listings, pick up a copy of the monthly *What's Up,* an excellent guide to all entertainment in Copenhagen, written in English and featuring a useful transport map on the back. It's free from various hotels, bars and cafés. *Where2go Copenhagen* is published twice a year and covers everything from design to shopping; the international editions are in English and are found in most hotels. The Visit Copenhagen Tourist Office is also very helpful: Gammel Kongevej 1. ☎ +45 3325 7400.

(*Cosmic Coaster, Under the Sea*), but you'll need to book ahead for the hour-long shows on the IMAX screen. *Gammel Kongevej 10.* ☎ *+45 3312 1224. www.tycho.dk. Tickets 125DKK includes two IMAX films. Bus 2A, 5A, 216. Map p 114.*

★★ **Palads** TIVOLI You can't fail to spot this brightly painted cinema complex near Tivoli. It is Copenhagen's biggest, with 17 screens. International blockbusters are shown in their native language with Danish subtitles. *Axeltorv 9.* ☎ *+45 7013 1211.www.palads123.dk.*

Tickets 30DKK–65DKK. Bus 2A, 5A, 15. Map p 114.

Opera

★★★ Det Kongelige Teater Operaen (Opera House)

DOKØEN Henning Larson's masterly opera house, is reputed to have perfect acoustics. It has become the Danish turf of international opera stars and runs major-league productions of *La Traviata* and *Der Rosenkavalier* in addition to experimental works chamber and symphony concerts. Smaller-scale

Entrance to the Rundetårn.

The Forum, venue for concerts and trade fairs.

productions take place on the Takkelloft, the second stage in the complex. *Ekvipagemestervej 10. ☎ +45 3369 6933. www.operaen.dk. Tickets around 100DKK for Main Stage, 40DKK–70DKK for Takkelloft. Boat: Harbor boat service from Nyhavn. Map p 114.*

Rock Venues

★★ Forum FREDERIKSBERG The Forum is a purpose-built venue with capacity for 10,000 standing in the stadium. Concerts, trade fairs and fashion shows are held here. *Thomsens Plads 1. ☎ +45 3247 2000. www.forumcopenhagen.dk. Tickets 110DKK–370DKK. Metro: Forum. Map p 114.*

★★ Plænen (Open-air Stage Tivoli) TIVOLI Regular Friday Rock concerts are held over the summer at the open-air stage smack in the middle of Tivoli (see p 10). Take wet-weather gear if it's raining—there's no shelter. *Tivoli Ticket Office, Vesterbrogade 3. ☎ +45 3312 1012. www.billetnet.dk. Ticket prices vary. Bus: 2A, 5A, 15. Map p 114.*

★★ Parken ØSTERBRO Denmark's national stadium has played host to many rock stalwarts (Stones, Springsteen, Elton John) and is also the home of FC Copenhagen (see p 122). Crowd capacity is 40,000. *Øster Alle 50. ☎ +45 3543 3131. www.parken.dk. Ticket prices vary. Train: Østerport. Map p 114.*

Sailing

★★ Copenhagen SWAN Challenge & Open World Championships SKOVSHOVED Surrounded by the calm, sheltered waters of the Øresund, it is small wonder Copenhageners take to the waters in droves. This event kicks off the Baltic SWAN Challenge and takes place over four days, usually at the beginning of June. July's Open World Championships guarantees fast-action fun for all the family as boats

Yachting is something of a national obsession.

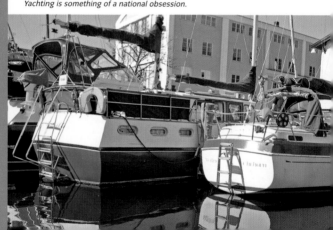

Det Kongelige Teater (Old Stage) dominates Kongens Nytorv, Copenhagen's grandest square.

battle for the wind. There are smaller regattas all summer long. *The Royal Danish Yacht Club, Rungsted Havn 42.*

☎ *+45 4586 8757. www.balticsea challenge.dk. Bus 14. Map p 114.*

Copenhagen Summertime

Scandinavia's hippest city goes into festival overdrive in summer; Copenhagen Distortion (www.cphdistortion.dk) kicks off with the biggest clubbing session of the year, with the **Jazz Festival** (www. festival.jazz.dk) close on its heels in July. The **Copenhagen International Ballet Festival** (www.copenhageninternationalballet.com) and a celebration of modern dance by Tim Rushton (see p 159) roll into town in August. It's the turn of the **Copenhagen Film Festival** to keep things lively in September (www. copenhagenfilmfestival.com). Out of town, July's four-day **Roskilde Festival** (www.roskilde-festival.dk) is one of the biggest in Europe; attracting mainstream acts. Hamlet and other characters pay homage to Shakespeare (www.hamletsommer.dk) in the courtyard of Kronborg Castle in Helsingør during July and August. For further information about Copenhagen festivals, see p 158.

Kronborg Castle courtyard, scene of Helsingør's Hamlet Summer Festival.

Det Kongelige Teater Skuespilhuset.

Soccer

★★ FC Copenhagen ØSTERBRO Copenhagen's soccer team play from Parken, the stadium also used for mainstream rock concerts (see p 120). Playing at home in an all-white strip, they were winners of the Danish league in 2007 and they have a considerable passionate following. *Øster Alle 50.* ☎ *+45 3543 7400. www.fck.dk. Ticket prices vary. Train: Østerport. Map p 114.*

Theater

★★★ Det Kongelige Teater (Old Stage) KONGENS NYTORV Sharing the same umbrella as the **Skuespilhuset** (see below) and Operaen (see p 119) the daddy of Danish theater puts on ballet performances and Sunday afternoon concerts. Performances in this fresco-ceilinged theater, built in 1748, are glamorous affairs, drawing a well-attired audience. *Kongens Nytorv 2.* ☎ *+45 3369 6933. www. kglteater.dk. Ticket prices vary. Metro: Kongens Nytorv. Map p 114.*

★★★ Det Kongelige Teater Skuespilhuset (Royal Danish Playhouse) NYHAVN Opened to great fanfare in February 2008, the playhouse stole the architectural thunder from its fellow institution, the Operaen (see p 119) across the Øresund. Designed by Danish firm Lundgård & Tranberg, the spectacularly squat building incorporates three stages, a tinted glass waterfront foyer, restaurant and a wide wooden boardwalk, perfect for a spot of sun bathing. Performances of *Hamlet* and Ingmar Bergman's *Høstsonaten* have been staged here. *Sankt Annæ Plads 36.* ☎ *+45 3369 6933. www.skuespilhus.dk. Ticket prices vary. Metro: Kongens Nytorv. Map p 114.*

★★ Teatret ved Sorte Hest (Black Horse Theater) VESTER-BRO This compact theater, tucked away in an old coach house, has garnered attention for introducing new stars to the Copenhagen arts firmament. Currently there are five avant-garde productions per year, mainly in Danish. *Vesterbrogade 150.* ☎ *+45 3331 0606. www.teatretved sortehest.dk. Ticket prices vary. Bus 2A, 5A, 216. Map p 114.* ●

Copenhagen Lodging

ØSTERBRO

Biesgdammvej
Fredensgade
Ryesgade
Ryesgade
Ryesgade
Ole Suhrs Gade

Sortedam Dossering
Sortedams Sø
Sortedams Sø

Øster Søgade
Øster Søgade
Øster Søgade
Øster Farimagsgade
Øster Farimagsgade

Solvgade
Stockholmsgade
Øster Farimagsgade

Holmens
Cemetery
Upsalagade

Visbygade
Oslo Plads
Østbanegade
Østbanegade

Folke Bernadottes Allé

Gernersgade
Grønningen

Østre
Anlæg's
Denmark's
National Gallery

Delfingade
Gernersgade
Skt Pauls Gade

Copenhagen
University
Solvgade

Fredericiagade
Klerkegade
Adelgade
Store Kongensgade
Borgergade

Bredgade

Copenhagen
University
Gothersgade

Botanisk
Have

Øster Voldgade

Rosenborg
Castle

King's
Gardens
Gothersgade

Frederiksborggade
tendersgade

Israels
Plads

Frederiksborggade

Landemærket
Kærboderne

Kronprinsessegade
Adelgade
Borgergade

Kronprinsensgade
Antonigade

Skt. Anne Plads

Ørsteds
Parken

Nørre Voldgade
Nørregade

Fiolstræde

Nørre Voldgade

THE LATIN
QUARTER

University

Skindergade
Købmagergade

CITY

Strøget
Amagertorv
Østergade

Kongens
Nytorv

Nyhavn

The Royal
Theatre

Herluf

Studiestræde
Rådhusstræde
Læderstræde
Højbro
Plads
Dybensgade

Niels Juels Gade

Vestergade
Domhuset
Kompagnistræde

Holmens Kanal

National
banken

Havnegade

City Hall
Square

City
Hall

Stormgade
Frederiksholms Kanal

Christiansborg

Slotsholmsgade
Bersgade

Knippelsbro

Strandgade
Wildersgade
Torvegade

Vesterbrogade

Tivoli

Dansk
Design
Centre

National
Museum

Vester Voldgade

Tøjhusgade

Christians Brygge

Jewish
Museum

The Royal
Library

CHRISTIANSHAVN

Tivoli
Concert
Hall

H C Andersens Boulevard

Tietgensgade
Bernstorffsgade

Glyptoteket

The Black
Diamond

Central
Station

Hammerichsgade

Kalvebod Brygge

Langebro
Christians Brygge

Langebrogade

Kalvebod
Bastion

Enhjørningens
Bastion

Panterens
Bastion

Stadsgraven

Kalvebod Brygge

SYDHAVNEN

Havne
Parken

Islands Brygge
Thorshavnsgade
Klaksvigsgade

Amager Boulevard
Weidekampsgade

Njalsgade
Artillerivej

(off map)

ISLANDS
BRYGGE

Lodging Best Bets

Hotel Nimb.

Most **Palatial Hotel**
★★★ D'Angleterre $$$$$ *Kongens Nytorv 34 (p 130)*

Best **Boutique Hotel & Spa**
★★★ Axel Hotel Guldsmeden $$$ *Helgolandsgade 7–11 (p 128)*

Best **Funky Art Hotel**
★★ Fox $$$ *Jarmers Plads 3 (p 131)*

Best for **Fashionistas**
★★★ Twentyseven $$$$ *Løngangstræde 27 (p 133)*

Best **Styled Rooms**
★★★ FRONT $$$$ *Sankt Annæ Plads 21 (p 131)*

Best for **Fireside Romance**
★★★ Avenue $$$ *Åboulevard 29 (p 128)*

Best for **Wealthy Stylistas**
★★ Sankt Petri $$$$$ *Krystalgade 22 (p 133)*

Best **Self-Catering**
★★★ Adina Apartment Hotel $$$ *Amerika Plads 7 (p 127)*

Smartest **Hotel Close to Tivoli**
★★ Alexandra $$$ *H C Andersens Boulevard 8 (p 127)*

Best **Seaside Views**
★★★ Marienlyst $$$$ *Nordre Strandvej 2, Helsingør (p 134)*

Best **Copenhagen Landmark**
★★ Radisson SAS Royal $$$$$ *Hammerichsgade 1 (p 132)*

Best **Views of the Opera House**
★★ Admiral $$$$ *Toldbodgade 24 (p 127)*

Best **Old-world English Charm**
★★★ Kong Frederik $$$$ *Vester Voldgade 25 (p 131)*

Best **Hotel in a Moorish Palace**
★★★ Nimb $$$$ *Bernstorffsgade 5 (p 132)*

Only **Hotel along Nyhavn**
★★ 71 Nyhavn $$$$ *Nyhavn 71 (p 127)*

Best **Budget Hotel**
★★ Savoy $$ *Vesterbrogade 34 (p 133)*

Best **Hostel**
★★★ Sleep-in Heaven $ *Struensee-gade 7 (p 133)*

Best **Gay B&B**
★★ Copenhagen Rainbow $ *Frederiksberggade 25c (p 130)*

Best **Family Hotel**
★★ Christian IV $$ *Dronningens Tværgade 45 (p 129)*

Best for **Business Travelers**
★★★ Radisson SAS Scandinavia $$$$ *Amager Boulevard 70 (p 132)*

Copenhagen Lodging A to Z

★★ **71 Nyhavn** NYHAVN In pole position as the only hotel along party-loving Nyhavn, 71 is a soothing mixture of contemporary style and original features in two superbly renovated gabled warehouses. Rooms are decorated in neutral colors and some have harbor or canal views. If you can't summon up the energy to explore Nyhavn (see p 7), the hotel restaurant Pakhushælderen serves up a mean Danish/French fusion menu. *Nyhavn 71.* ☎ *+45 3343 6200. www. 71nyhavnhotel.com. 150 units. Doubles 1195DKK–1995DKK w/breakfast. AE, DC, MC, V. Metro: Kongens Nytorv. Map p 124.*

★★★ kids **Adina Apartment Hotel** NORDHAVN The cool Adina is a 15-minute hike along pretty Langelinie north of the city center and based at the glossy development near the ferry terminal. This is currently Copenhagen's top hotel of choice with stylish, modern apartments combined with top-notch facilities including a pool, gym, and restaurant. Ask for a seventh-floor room for great views over the city. *Amerika plads 7.* ☎ *+45 3969 1000. www.adina.dk. 128 units. 1050DKK–1550DKK. AE, MC, V. Train: S-Tog to Østerport. Map p 124.*

★★ **Admiral** NYHAVN A venerable old boy on the Copenhagen hotel scene, the Admiral stretches along the waterfront in a warehouse dating from 1787. The interior is crammed with original pine beams, and a nautical theme runs through the ground floor; guest rooms are decorated with teak and those at the front of the hotel have a bird's-eye view of the Opera House (see p 119). The hotel is also home to SALT restaurant (see p 100), a true gastronomic treat in a brick-vaulted dining room. *Toldbodgade 24.* ☎ *+45 3374 1414. www.admiralhotel.dk. 366 units. Doubles 1510DKK–1750DKK. AE, DC, MC, V. Metro: Kongens Nytorv. Map p 124.*

★★ GREEN **Alexandra** RÅDHUS-PLADSEN The lobby at the Alexandra is decked out with stylish Danish furniture and art while 13 'design' rooms feature chairs by such illustrious Danish furniture designers as Finn Juhl and Arne Jacobsen, among

The Admiral, an ex-warehouse on the Øresund.

others. Light sleepers should reserve standard rooms at the back of the hotel rather than the plush 'design' rooms that overlook noisy Rådhuspladsen. One floor is now equipped with anti-allergy bedding, giving the place a coveted Green Key award for environmental considerations. *H C Andersens Boulevard 8.* ☎ *+45 3374 4444. www.hotel-alexandra.dk. 61 units. Doubles 1425DKK–2125DKK w/breakfast. AE, MC, V. Bus 2A, 5A, 151. Map p 124.*

★ **Ascot** TIVOLI   Expect to be greeted at the door of the Ascot by staff wearing full Danish national costume. Inside the rooms are spotless and reasonably sized for Copenhagen. Tivoli is only a short walk away, but if you feel like staying in, you'll find an array of restaurants in-house; the Reef 'n' Turf serves up an unusual menu of bush foods such as Australian kangaroo and vegemite-flavored steak. If you're not in the mood for wattle seeds and desert peaches, however, there are tapas and Italian eateries elsewhere in the hotel. *Studiestræde 61.* ☎ *+45 3312 6000. www. ascot-hotel.dk. 120 units. Doubles 1190DKK–1890DKK w/breakfast. AE, MC, V. Bus 2A, 5A, 151. Map p 124.*

★★★ GREEN **Axel Hotel Guldsmeden** VESTERBRO   A stylish, Balinese-influenced addition to the excellent Guldsmeden portfolio of Danish hotels (see also Carlton Hotel, p 129). Rooms have four-poster beds and tiny, but perfectly constructed, tiled bathrooms with showers and luxury toiletries. Most food and drink is organic, the chunky crockery is FairTrade, and there is a beautifully designed spa tucked in the basement. *Helgolandsgade 7–11.* ☎ *+45 3331 3266. www. hotelguldsmeden.com. 129 units. Doubles 1615DKK–1995DKK. AE, DC, MC, V. Bus 2A, 5A, 216. Map p 124.*

★★★ kids **Avenue** FREDERIKSBERG   Indisputably my favorite Copenhagen hotel for its relaxed, chilled atmosphere. The Avenue welcomes guests with roaring open fires, flickering candles, a well-stocked bar, board games, and a library—it's a real home-from-home. Rooms are spacious and soothingly decorated in a pale palette, with pristine white-tiled bathrooms. A limited but tasty menu of classics such as tapas and Caesar salads are served throughout the day in the bar. There's also a suntrap terrace at

The comfortable lounge at Avenue Hotel.

the back, and parking for 28 cars. Free Wi-Fi. *Åboulevard 29.* ☎ *+45 3537 3111. www.avenuehotel.dk. 68 units. Doubles 1175DKK–1625DKK w/breakfast. AE, DC, MC, V. Metro: Forum. Map p 124.*

★★★ **Cabinn City** TIVOLI Certainly not a luxury destination but what you *do* get in this purpose-built, low-cost concept hotel is a serviceable room with private bathroom and free internet access. Breakfast and parking are optional extras. If you're happy with the basics and don't expect to be pampered, this is a good bet in a generally very pricey city. *Mitchellsgade 14.* ☎ *+45 3346 1616. www.cabinn. com. 352 units. Doubles 665DKK. MC, V. Bus: 2A, 5A, 15l. Map p 124.*

★★ kids GREEN **Camping Charlottenlund Fort** CHARLOTTEN-LUND Situated by a long, sandy beach on the Øresund and a mere 6km from the center of Copenhagen, this campsite is ideal for families who want the great outdoors combined with city sightseeing. Tents, caravans, and mobile homes are all welcome and the site's facilities encompass functional, communal restrooms, laundry, hot-dog stands, and an on-site fast-food restaurant. Kids love the pedalos and bouncy castle and as the sea is virtually tideless, it is safe for swimming. Pony trekking nearby. Apr–Sep. *Strandvejen 144B, Charlottenlund.* ☎ *+45 3962 3688. www. campingcopenhagen.dk. 98 units. From 35DKK. 6km north of Copenhagen. MC, V. Bus no. 14 runs to Copenhagen center every 10–20 mins. Map p 124.*

★★ **Carlton Hotel Guldsmeden** VESTERBRO If you're seeking a bargain but don't want to sacrifice on style, then the Carlton provides the solution. Another of the chic Guldsmeden chain owned by Marc and Sandra Weinert, located in edgy

Vesterbro. Rooms are decorated in French Colonial style with teak four-poster beds, gilt mirrors and Persian rugs. The breakfast menu is largely organic. Parking at the back. *Vesterbrogade 66.* ☎ *+45 3322 1500. www. hotelguldsmeden.com. 64 units. Doubles 1045DKK–1180DKK. AE, DC, MC, V. Bus 2A, 5A, 216. Map p 124.*

★★ kids **Christian IV** FRED-ERIKSSTADEN A small, family-run hotel in a quiet backwater, this is an ideal base for families with children who can run off energy in the nearby Kongens Have park (see p 86). The rooms are starkly decorated in grays and blues, with sharply contrasting scarlet wall hangings and curtains, but there is a generous buffet breakfast and the cheery staff will advise on nearby eating options. *Dronningens Tværgade 45.* ☎ *+45 3332 1044. www.hotelchristianiv.dk. 42 units. Doubles 1125DKK–1215DKK w/breakfast. MC, V. Metro: Kongens Nytorv. Map p 124.*

★★ **Citi let** STRØGET Groups of up to six travelers can find considerable savings in these sleek and trendy apartments, all in central locations and to let for a minimum of a month. They come complete with daily maid service, cable TV, phones, and Wi-Fi as well as immaculate designer-standard kitchens and bathrooms. *Fortunstræde 4.* ☎ *+45 7022 2129. www.citilet.dk. Apartments 7,000DKK–15,000DKK. AE, MC, V. Map p 124.*

★ **Comfort Hotel Esplanaden** FREDERIKSSTADEN Much the better of the two Comfort hotels near Østerport (the other is next to the railway tracks). Plainly furnished with high-ceilinged rooms in muted blues and browns, the Esplanaden's main selling point is its privileged proximity to many of Copenhagen's major sights; the Little Mermaid (see p 59), Resistance Museum (see p 58), Art and Design Museum (see p 16), Amalienborg Palace (see p 41) and the exclusive shops of Bredgade are within easy striking distance on foot. Nip round the corner for *smørrebrød* at Café Petersborg (see p 94). *Bredgade 78.* ☎ *+45 3348 1000. www.choicehotels. no. 117 units. Doubles 895DKK–1895DKK. AE, MC, V. Metro: Kongens Nytorv. Map p 124.*

★★ Copenhagen Marriott

TIVOLI A luxurious chain hotel with a wonderful position overlooking the waters of Sydhavnen. Plenty of business travelers pass through to use the extensive meeting facilities, but holidaymakers will be happy enough with the gleaming health club, views of Copenhagen from the sunny Terraneo Terrace, and the spacious, elegantly furnished guest rooms. *Kalvebod Brygge 5.* ☎ *+45 8833 9900. www.marriott.com/hotels/ travel/cphdk-copenhagen-marriott-hotel. 401 units. Doubles 1799DKK–2499DKK. AE, DC, MC, V. Bus 2A, 5A, 151. Map p 124.*

★★★ Copenhagen Rainbow

RÅDHUSPLADSEN A small, privately run, and gay-friendly B&B on the top floor of a tall, thin 19th-century building at the raucous end of Strøget (see p 8). The rooms are functional but spotless (two share a shower) and there's a shared kitchen and a well-equipped lounge for communal breakfasts. *Frederiksberggade 25C.* ☎ *+45 3314 1020. www. copenhagen-rainbow.dk. 5 units. Doubles 790DKK–995DKK w/breakfast. Bus 2A, 5A, 151. Map p 124.*

★★★ D'Angleterre KONGENS

NYTORV Dominating Copenhagen's buzzing main square, this palatial hotel is synonymous with luxury and sophistication. Opened in 1855, it is presently under the auspices of NP Hotels, who are restoring the magnificent public areas. The well-appointed rooms are carefully furnished with traditional Danish pieces, and suites come in four levels of opulence, with prices to match. There's a glamorous restaurant and the basement spa is run by the Danish fitness guru, Lotte Arndal. *Kongens Nytorv 34.* ☎ *+45 3312 0095. www.dangleterre.com. 123 units. Doubles 3125DKK–5650DKK. AE, DC, MC, V. Metro: Kongens Nytorv. Map p 124.*

Hotel D'Angleterre.

★★ Fox RÅDHUSPLADSEN Each room in the eccentric Fox is wildly decorated by avant-garde artists in a hotch-potch of styles, so look at the website for an idea of the options beforehand. Breakfast is served in reception and is somewhat sparse—everything is served in glasses, which is fine for coffee and yogurt but not so clever for pancakes. The Tiki bar Intoxica (see p 109) fills to the gunnels nightly with chic Copenhagen stylistas. *Jarmers Plads 3.* ☎ *+45 3313 3000. www.hotelfox.dk. 61 units. Doubles 1690DKK–1990DKK. MC, V. Bus: 2A, 5A, 151. Map p 124.*

★★★ FRONT NYHAVN Part of the top-class NP Hotels chain along with D'Angleterre (see p 130) and Kong Frederik (see p 131). and one of the best-value stays in town. Black lacquered furniture, plum bed throws, plasma screens and quality white linen combine with classy bathrooms in pale shades. Ask for a room overlooking the Øresund and Operaen (see p 119). Downstairs there is a small gym, and breakfast is served in the bar, which doubles as an American-style diner at night (see p 97). *Sankt Annæ Plads 21.* ☎ *+45 3313 3400. www.front.dk. 132 units. Doubles 1940DKK–2980DKK. AE, DC, MC, V. Metro: Kongens Nytorv. Map p 124.*

★★ Grand Hotel Copenhagen VESTERBRO One of Arp-Hansen's nine Copenhagen hotels and found in a pastel-painted mansion dating back to 1890. The rooms come in six sizes from 'tourist' to suite; don't be tempted by the tiny savings price-wise on the tourist rooms because space-wise they are tiny too. Service and room décor is all a bit plain but location is all; the Grand is close to the Wonderful Copenhagen tourist office, Tivoli, and the train station, with easy access to the airport. There's also a decent Italian restaurant, Frascati, often full of business travelers. *Vesterbrogade 9.* ☎ *+45*

3327 6900. www.grandhotel copenhagen.com. 161 units. Doubles 1195DKK–1475DKK w/breakfast. AE, DC, MC, V. Bus: 2A, 5A, 216. Map p 124.*

★ Hilton Copenhagen Airport KASTRUP Bland and functional the rooms may be, but this Hilton is connected to the airport's Terminal 3 and so is the perfect pit-stop for travelers on overnight trips. It's a 20-minute metro journey right to all the main sights of the city, so you can dine out in central Copenhagen and get back to the hotel in time for a last drink in the swish Axis Lounge. Too tired to move? There's also a pool and spa. *Ellehammersvej 20.* ☎ *+45 3250 1501. www.hilton.co.uk/ copenhagen. 60 units. Doubles 1375DKK–3645DKK. AE, DC, MC, V. Metro: Kastrup. Map p 124.*

★★ GREEN Kong Arthur NØRREPORT In a handsome 18th-century building and transformed into a CO_2-neutral environment, this is the best of four Brøchner hotels in Copenhagen. The bedrooms are jauntily decked out with striped bedspreads in pastel hues and carefully chosen artwork. In the summer, you can enjoy a beer or breakfast on the little terrace. Free access to the soothing spa and the location in trendy, café-filled Nørreport add to the manifold attractions of this convivial hotel. *Nørre Søgade 11.* ☎ *+45 3311 1212. www.kongarthur.dk. 155 units. Doubles 1505DKK–1750DKK w/breakfast. AE, MC, V. Metro: Nørreport. Map p 124.*

★★ Kong Frederik RÅDHUSPLADSEN Housed in an ancient building tucked away from the din of Rådhuspladsen, Kong Frederik retains the air of an old-fashioned English country hotel. There are creaking corridors, hunting prints, chintzy bedroom furniture, wood-paneled walls, and a flower-filled courtyard on the ground floor. Its award-winning Coq Rouge brasserie serves mussels and steak, and the cozy little bar does brisk daily business. *25 Vester Voldgade. ☎ +45 3312 5902. www.nphotels.dk/ kongfrederik. 110 units. Doubles 1490DKK–2210DKK. AE, DC, MC, V. Bus 2A, 5A, 151. Map p 124.*

★ **Le Méridien Palace** RÅDHUS-PLADSEN   The grand old lady of Rådhuspladsen was renovated in 2008 after a take-over by Le Méridien Group. The new look is sharp and contemporary in style, although some rooms are tiny. Still, it's at the heart of Copenhagen's busiest square and right opposite Tivoli; this too has its drawbacks—traffic by day and reveling Danes by night. *Rådhuspladsen 57. ☎ +45 3314 4050. www.palace hotel.dk. 166 units. Doubles 1360DKK– 3060DKK w/breakfast. AE, DC, MC, V. Bus 2A, 5A, 151. Map p 124.*

★ **Maritime** KONGENS NYTORV   Quietly located in a residential street a step away from Nyhavn, this unassuming place has brightly decorated if slightly spartan rooms and old-fashioned bathrooms, all with showers. It's reasonable value for the center of Copenhagen if you don't mind the simple accommodations. *Peder Skrams Gade 19. ☎ +45 3313 4882. www.hotel-maritime.dk. 64 units. Doubles 850DKK–1900DKK. MC, V. Metro: Kongens Nytorv. Map p 124.*

★★★ **Nimb** TIVOLI   The much-vaunted arrival of Copenhagen's latest boutique hotel has not disappointed; the 13 individually designed luscious suites, all with antique furniture and open fires, have proved an instant hit with fashion-conscious travelers. The food at gourmet restaurant Herman (see p 98) is attracting praise for head chef Herman and there's the Nimb bistro (see p 80) for less formal dining. Combine all that with great views over Tivoli and this place is a sure-fire winner, albeit an expensive one.

Bernstorffsgade 5. ☎ +45 8870 0000. www.nimb.dk. 13 units. Doubles 2900DKK–8500DKK. AE, DC, MC, V. Bus 2A, 5A, 151. Map p 124.

★ **Phoenix Copenhagen** FRED-ERIKSSTADEN   The glamorous big sister of the Grand (see p 131) boasts a fine 17th-century home in gentrified Bredgade. Redolent of a mini-Versailles inside, the rooms and public spaces may be a little too gilded for some tastes, and the suites are positively over the top, but the overall impression is one of refined gentility from a bygone age. There's a sleek French restaurant and an ersatz English pub. *Bredgade 37. ☎ +45 3395 9500. www.phoenix copenhagen.dk. 213 units. Doubles 995DKK–1805DKK w/breakfast. AE, DC, MC, V. Metro: Kongens Nytorv. Map p 124.*

★ **Radisson SAS Royal** TIVOLI   Copenhagen's iconic and original skyscraper hotel was designed from top to toe by Arne Jacobsen (see p 29) and is visible all over the city. There are Egg chairs in the foyer, a devilishly beautiful twisted spiral staircase, and elements of his work in all the guest rooms, all of which have contemporary technologies such as free broadband. Suite 606 contains original Jacobsen pieces; he hated many of his creations for the hotel and refused to use the cutlery. Reserve tables for dinner at the Alberto K—the views across the city are spectacular. *Hammerichsgade 1. ☎ +45 3342 6000. www.royal. copenhagen.radissonsas.com. 260 units. Doubles 1895DKK–2095DKK w/breakfast. AE, DC, MC, V. Bus 2A, 5A, 151. Map p 124.*

★★ **Radisson SAS Scandinavia** AMAGER   Close to the train station and 15 minutes from the airport, Copenhagen's premier business hotel has facilities for small informal meetings right up to conferences holding 3,000 delegates. Junior suites and business-class rooms enjoy great views towards Nyhavn but most appealing are the 'urban-themed' standard-grade bedrooms with chunky glass walls behind the beds and good-sized bathrooms. Four restaurants, including the gourmet Dining Room on the 25th floor, and a fitness center complete the sleek package. Free Internet in rooms. *Amager Boulevard 70.* ☎ *+45 3815 6500. www.radissonsas.com. 542 units. Doubles 1895DKK–2295DKK w/breakfast. AE, DC, MC, V. Metro: Amagerbro; Train: Islands Brygge; Bus: 5a, 33. Map p 124.*

★★★ kids **Sankt Petri** LATIN QUARTER A renovated warehouse with star quality, this vibrant member of First Hotels claims to provide Copenhagen's hippest accommodation. The guestrooms are perfectly appointed, as befits a five-star establishment, but it's the enormous lobby that grabs attention; a huge black reception desk, walls scattered with artwork, and contemporary furniture. Dine in at funky Asian restaurant Bleu or hang out in Bar Rouge (see p 109), which attracts a moneyed smart crowd at the weekend. There's also a sun terrace and plunge pool at the back of the hotel. *Krystalgade 22.* ☎ *+45 3345 9100. www.hotelskt petri.com. 268 units. Doubles 1495DKK–2895DKK w/breakfast. AE, DC, MC, V. Metro: Nørreport. Map p 124.*

★★ **Savoy** VESTERBRO It's the Savoy but not as we know it. This version is a bargain hotel in a brilliant location just off Rådhuspladsen. The rooms are plainly furnished along clean Scandinavian lines, all with windows overlooking a peaceful internal courtyard. Choose a top-floor room for sloping ceilings and views over the city rooftops. *Vesterbrogade 34.* ☎ *+45 3326 7500. www. savoyhotel.dk. 66 units. Doubles 895DKK–1095DKK w/breakfast. MC, V. Bus 2A, 5A, 216. Map p 124.*

★★ **Sleep-in Heaven** NØRREBRO Buzzy hostel with dorms and some scarily high three-story bunks. Open 24 hours and mostly the spotless preserve of backpackers. *Struenseegade 7.* ☎ *+45 3535 4648. www. sleepinheaven.com. 80 units. Dormitory beds 172DKK. MC, V. Bus: 250s. Map p 124.*

★★★ **Twentyseven** RÅDHUS-PLADSEN A bastion of cool; well placed near the major museums. Staff members are unbelievably hip and helpful and the rooms (ask for one at the back of the hotel if you want to sleep beyond 5.30am) are designed in smart reds and white, complete with inky-black bathrooms. A delicious tapas-style supper is included in the price of your stay, served in the Wine Room, where 40 different vintages are on tap for tasting. The Honey Rider Cocktail Lounge (see p 109) does a roaring trade, and for an ice-cold night out, visit the Absolut Ice Bar (see p 108) across the courtyard. *Løngangstræde 27.* ☎ *+45 7027 5627. www.hotel27.dk. 200 units. Doubles 1395DKK–1895DKK*

The stylish dining room at Twentyseven.

w/breakfast. MC, V. Bus 2A, 5A, 151. Map p 124.

Helsingør

★★ kids Bretagne HELSINGØR

Peacefully hidden away and overlooking the lake at Hornbæk on the north coast of Zealand, the Bretagne is a stone's throw from Helsingør (see p 149) and ideal for a night of R&R. Inside this whitewashed mansion (it started life as a hospital) the rooms are traditionally furnished but with strange twists; in one room there is a kitsch mural of the lake behind the bed. Prices are reasonable and the Brünniche restaurant is pretty decent in a nouvelle-cuisine style. *Sauntevej 18, Hornbæk, Helsingør.* ☎ *+45 4970 1666. www.hotelbretagne.dk. 26 units. Doubles 825DKK–1395DKK. MC, V. Train: Helsingør. 50km north of Copenhagen. Map p 124.*

★★★ kids Marienlyst HELSINGØR

With marvelous views across the Øresund to Sweden, this splendid seaside hotel has an atmosphere reminiscent of times past. Families make good use of the indoor pool, slides, and splash pools or swim off the strip of sandy beach. A recent

Looking over the dining rooms at Hotel Marienlyst.

overhaul has seen the bar transformed by dark, moody tones, and the bathrooms updated in natural hues. There are two restaurants and a casino full of smartly dressed thirty-somethings. *Nordre Strandvej 2, Helsingør.* ☎ *+45 4921 4000. www. marienlyst.dk. 222 units. Doubles 1395DKK–1850DKK w/breakfast. AE, DC, MC, V. Train: Helsingør. 50km north of Copenhagen. Map p 124.*

Hillerød

Hillerød HILLERØD   Just about the only option for an overnight stay in Hillerød after visiting romantic Frederiksborg Castle (see p 143). This hotel purports to be four star but in reality it is little more than a motel. However it has all the facilities; basic but well-equipped bedrooms and a cafeteria-style restaurant and suffices for an overnight stay. *Milnersvej 41.* ☎ *+45 4824 0874. Hotelhillerod.dk. 113 units. Doubles 1160DKK– 1260DKK w/breakfast. MC, V. Train: Hillerød. 32km north-west of Copenhagen. Map p 124.*

Roskilde

★★★ Prindsen ROSKILDE   Quite

an unconventional but endearing find in Roskilde, with an ornate Golden Age banqueting hall that was first used in 1880. Even the standard rooms are spacious and well designed, with free internet access and writing desk, while the memory of Hans Christian Andersen's several visits is evoked in the eponymous suite, traditionally laid out with antique wooden furniture. The Brasserie restaurant—adorned with some much talked-about still life paintings—serves decent food. *Algade 13, Roskilde.* ☎ *+45 4630 9100. www.hotelprindsen.dk. 76 units. Doubles 1600DKK–1815DKK w/breakfast. MC, V. Train: Roskilde. 25km north-west of Copenhagen. Map p 124.* ●

Arken, Museum for Modern Art

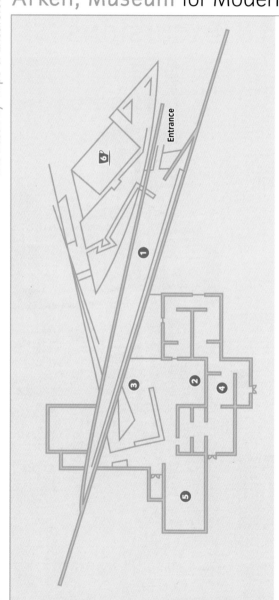

Entrance

Southwest of Copenhagen, Arken is housed in an extraordinary building designed by Danish architect Søren Robert Lund, and when viewed from the right spot, it resembles a ship looming out of the sea. Take a half-day trip (two to three hours) to see this collection of ground-breaking contemporary art or combine Arken with a visit to the beach at Ishøj Strand for a fun, family day out. **START: Follow the E20 17km from the center of Copenhagen and take exit 26 to Ishøj Strand. By rail, take S-trains A or E from Hovedbanegården (Central Station) to Ishøj. From there, bus 128 runs straight to the museum.**

1 ★★ Sculpture Galleries. Arken reopened in early 2008 following the addition of a new, light-flooded sculpture gallery, with installations on show from the permanent collection. Look out for Olafur Eliasson's *Light Ventilator Mobile*, illuminating with a searchlight and circulating air with four fans. Close by is Jeppe Hein's *Mirror Spiral Labyrinth*, which leads confused visitors around in circles.

2 ★★★ Damien Hirst Room. The biggest collection of Hirst's work in Scandinavia is for me the museum's biggest draw. See spot paintings and a sinister silk print of his infamous gem-encrusted skull, *For the Love of God*, scattered with sparkling diamond dust. More celebratory is *The Four Elements*, four colored blocks appropriately subtitled *Who's Afraid of Red, Yellow, Green and Blue?*

3 ★★★ Photographic Exhibition. There are some very moving images in the permanent collection,

especially Richard Billingham's evocative series of family shots. A favorite of mine is the massive *Bringing it All Back Home* by Claus Carstensen & Superflex; figures pose in scrubland wearing animal masks.

4 ★★★ Temporary Exhibitions. This gallery has featured some stunners in the past; works by the Skagen painters (Danish Impressionists, see p 25) and a surrealist exhibition with works by Dalí and Miró.

5 ★ Arken's Collection. Revolving exhibitions show off selections from the gallery's 300 pieces of contemporary Danish art after 1990. Look out for John Bock's messy installation *Redigging the Lumps* and Anselm Reyle's *Untitled*, evoking a kitsch Caribbean sunset.

6 ★★ kids Arken Café. has views of Køge Bay but if the weather is fine, head to the beach for a swim and picnic lunch.

Practical Matters: Arken

Admission to **Arken** is 85DKK, 70DKK concessions, children under 17 free, and you can use your Copenhagen Card (see p 8). There are English-speaking guided tours on Wednesday and Sunday; book in advance online. Skovvej 100, 2635 Ishøj. ☎ +45 4354 0222. www.arken.dk. Open Tues–Sun 10am–5pm; Wed 10am–9pm. Closed Mon.

Viking Ship Museum, Roskilde

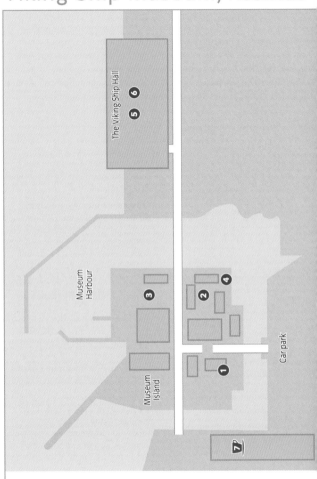

The Viking Ship Hall

Museum Harbour

Museum Island

Car park

- ❶ Archaeological Workshop
- ❷ Viking Meeting Place
- ❸ Boat Yard
- ❹ Boat Trips from the Harbor
- ❺ Viking Ship Hall
- ❻ Skuldelev Ships
- 7️⃣ Restaurant Snekken

An easy journey west from Copenhagen, Roskilde is perfect for a family day out at the Viking Ship Museum, a complex partly built on an island of reclaimed land on the edge of the fjord at Roskilde, itself an attractive old town full of historic buildings and with a traffic-free center. Its other claim to fame is the majestic Gothic cathedral, traditional burial place of the Danish Royal Family (see p 141). START: To travel the 30km to Roskilde by car, follow the E21 from the center of Copenhagen and take exit 11. The museum is signposted through the center of town. By rail, take S-train C from Hovedbanegården (Central Station) to Roskilde; they depart every 20 minutes and the journey takes half an hour. From there, bus no.s 216 or 607 run to the museum, or it's 20 minutes on foot.

Reconstructed Viking boats in the harbor.

1 ★ Archaeological Work-shop. Step into Museum Island's workshop to see the painstaking reconstruction work involved in restoring a 12th-century cargo ship called *Roskilde 4*, found just west of the museum in the fjord. Nine medieval wrecks were found around the bay when Museum Island was constructed in the 1990s.

2 ★ kids Viking Meeting Place (Tunet). A courtyard forming a hive of traditional Viking activity with workshops for kids; they can try coin minting, wood planning, and painting, or watch the blacksmith

(sadly not wearing his Viking helmet) heat his fire with bellows. Coopers and rope-makers are also hard at work, and there are archery demonstrations here in the summer.

3 ★★ kids Boat Yard. The craftsmen at this working boatyard make reconstructions of Viking and medieval designs by traditional methods; some of the boats are sailed from the adjacent harbor but many are sold overseas to provide an income for the museum. There's a mine of pictorial information in Danish and English around the yard, explaining each step of the

Partially restored longboat.

boat-building process, from selecting the wood to making the nails.

④ ★★★ kids Boat Trips from the Harbor. A 50-minute trip around Roskilde Fjord on a reconstructed square-sailed longboat gives you the chance to get that real Viking experience—but be warned—if there is no wind you'll have to row! It's fun even if the weather is doing its worst. Kids can dress in Viking clothes and have their pictures taken on the reconstructed cargo boats nearby. In summer, there are occasional evening boat trips to admire the late-setting sun.

⑤ ★ Viking Ship Hall. Across the wooden harbor bridge from Museum Island, the wonderfully designed and light-filled Viking Ship Hall has massive glass walls overlooking the fjord. This houses the museum's permanent exhibition and five reconstructed Viking longboats. One exhibition hall is dedicated to the voyages of *The Sea Stallion*, a replica longboat that sails between the museum and Glendalough in County Wicklow, Ireland. In the basement, a short film is shown in English, telling the Viking tale and summarizing the work of the museum. There's also a series of posters depicting the progress of an 11th-century raid on Roskilde from the sea.

⑥ ★★★ kids Skuldelev Ships. The absolute highlights of the museum, these five Viking wrecks were scuttled in the 11th century near Skuldelev, north of Roskilde, to provide a defense barrier against rival Viking raids. They lay there until they were excavated in 1962 in thousands of pieces. After a long period of reconstruction, the ships are now semi-intact, lurking in eerie

Practical Matters: Viking Ship Museum

Admission to the **Viking Ship Museum** is 95DKK (75DKK concessions, free kids under 17); Copenhagen Cards (see p 8) are not accepted. *Vindeboder 12, 4000 Roskilde.* ☎ *+45 4630 0200.* English-speaking guided tours, ☎ *+45 4630 0253. www.vikingeskibs museet.dk.* Boat trips 60DKK. Open daily 10am–5pm.

Domkirke—Royal Burial Place

You'll find Roskilde's splendid brick cathedral a few hundred meters up a steep hill from the **Viking Ship Museum**. There has been a church on the site since the 9th century, but this tall, austere Gothic incarnation was commissioned by Bishop Absalon, the founder of Copenhagen (see p 167), in the 1200s. It contains the tombs of most Danish royals since the Lutheran Reformation in 1536 to the present day. The opulent chapels off the main aisle house the elaborate sarcophagi of many Frederiks, Christians, and their queens. The remains of Harald Bluetooth, the 10th-century first Christian king of Denmark (see p 166), is buried in a pillar on the left of the sanctuary. Look for the wonderfully named 'tomb of the ghost horse' behind the sanctuary. The great gold altarpiece depicts Christ's trials in Holy Week and was made in Ghent in the 1560s. The latest royal incumbents of the cathedral are the parents of the present queen, who are buried in a new tomb in the gardens. *Domkirkepladsen, 4000 Roskilde.* ☎ *+45 4631 6565. www.roskildedomkirke.dk. Admission 25DKK,15DKK concessions. Jan 1–Mar 31 & Oct 1–Dec 31 Tues–Fri 10am–4pm; Sat 12.30pm–4pm. Apr 1–Sept 30 Mon 9am–4.45pm; Tues–Fri 9am–5pm; Sat 12.30pm–5pm. There are guided tours that take about one hour; for details contact* **Roskilde Tourist Information Bureau**; *Stændertorvet 1, 4000 Roskilde.* ☎ *+45 4631 6565. www.visitroskilde.com.*

splendor against the backdrop of the fjord. Made of oak, the fastest was *Skuldelev 2*, an ocean-going warship; 30 meters long and capable of speeds of up to 20 knots. She was built near Dublin somewhere around 1042. Of the others, two were trading vessels and one an inshore fishing boat.

7 ★★ **Restaurant Snekken.** A better option than the museum café (which serves pricey salads and lager), Snekken is by the entrance to the Viking Ship Museum. It has views across the fjord, fresh sushi during the day, and a quality brasserie menu in the evening. Booking is advisable, especially during school holidays. *Vindeboder 16, 4000 Roskilde.* ☎ *+45 4635 9816. www.snekken.dk. $$.*

The Gothic Roskilde Cathedral.

Frederiksborg Slot, Hillerød

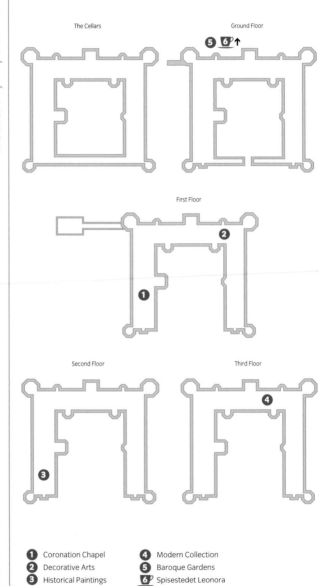

The Cellars

Ground Floor

First Floor

Second Floor

Third Floor

1 Coronation Chapel
2 Decorative Arts
3 Historical Paintings
4 Modern Collection
5 Baroque Gardens
6 Spisestedet Leonora

Gloriously romantic Frederiksborg Slot (Castle) is perched on a lake in Hillerød, an otherwise unassuming little town northwest of Copenhagen. Built in the early 17th century in the reign of Christian IV (see p 168), the copper roofs of this fairy-tale confection glisten in the sun. Built on three tiny islands, overlooking picture-perfect formal gardens, and entered through a cobbled courtyard with an extravagant central fountain, the rambling Dutch Renaissance palace contains Denmark's Museum of National History, founded by brewing magnate JC Jacobsen in 1878, an awesomely opulent chapel, magnificent public rooms, and a collection of modern portraits. START: By car from Copenhagen, take the E47 north and turn off at junction 9, signposted Hillerød; the journey is 38km. The castle is not well sign-posted but it's easy to spot when driving through the town. By rail, take S-train E from Hovedbanegården (Central Station) to Hillerød; they depart every 20 minutes and the journey takes 40 minutes. From there, it's a 20-minute walk (follow the little blue signposts) or a five-minute bus journey on routes 701, 702, 703, or 325 to the castle.

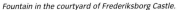

❶ ★★★ Coronation Chapel. Once in the castle, head for the vaulted Knights Room, reconstructed following the fire of 1859, which destroyed swathes of the original castle. From here, take the stairs up to the second-floor chapel, which escaped fire damage, and check out the eye-catching, gilded ceiling. Royal portraits adorn the walls and an ornate, world-famous organ by German master craftsman Esaias Campenius (1560–1617) installed in 1610 dominates the far end of the chapel. Add to this the jewel-like stained-glass windows and you have a riot of color fit for the coronation of monarchs between 1671 and 1840. On leaving the chapel, make sure you see the baroque Audience Chamber, where a hatch in the floor reveals the throne used to lift the king into the room. It's down a corridor with a carved marble ceiling and entered through marble curtains held back by cherubs.

Fountain in the courtyard of Frederiksborg Castle.

Campenius's organ in the chapel.

2 ★ Decorative Arts. Wander through the magnificent state rooms on the third floor of the castle and you'll spy Delft pottery, spindly rococo furniture and Flemish tapestries hanging on the walls. Wherever you go, you'll see heavily decorated ceilings and elaborately patterned marbled floors. The ceiling of Room 31 depicts the night sky in bright blues and golds, while Room 36 is laid out for a ghostly dinner party, complete with scarlet walls and cardboard cutouts of bewigged gentlemen. They are watched over by a series of oil paintings of past kings and queens. The impressive Great Hall (Room 38) has an intricate marble floor and ceiling decorated with cherubim, gilding and mythical

paintings; the room is laid out as it was in the time of Christian IV, chief architect of Copenhagen (see p 168). Room 39 houses the elaborate Celestial Globe (1657), ornamented with figures representing the 12 signs of the zodiac. Parts of the original Flora Danica dinner service (see right) are on display along with an eclectic collection of Danish-designed furniture of varying ages and styles.

3 ★ Historical Paintings. An impressive set of massive historical paintings showing seminal moments in Danish culture are scattered throughout the castle. Look at the walls of the Great Hall for mammoth-sized oils. A small selection of prints and drawings from a collection of over 40,000 is also on display, often depicting the castle.

4 ★ Modern Collection. On the creaky fourth floor of the castle, the modern collection contains many portraits of often-obscure Danes, but there are some important exceptions. One image of Queen Margrethe shows her elegantly attired, but oddly placed on a stool in the middle of a field. Another, very different take on the Queen is the surprisingly conventional portrait in profile by Andy Warhol. Look out for the self-portrait by Skagen painter Peter Severin Krøyer (see p 25), black-and-white

Practical Matters: Frederiksborg Castle

Admission to **Frederiksborg Castle** is 60DKK, 50DKK concessions; 15DKK children 6–15; 120DKK family ticket), and Copenhagen Cards (see p 8) are welcome. Labeling in English is scant. There are English guided tours; book in advance on the number below. *3400 Hillerød.* ☎ *+45 4826 0439. www.frederiksborgmuseet.dk.* Apr–Oct 10am–5pm; Nov–Mar 11am–3pm.

Flora Danica

Royal Copenhagen's most exquisite porcelain design came into being in 1790 when Christian VII's brother commissioned the company to produce a china service that would impress Empress Catherine II of Russia, who was being wooed as a potential royal bride. She died in 1796 before the service was finished, and so it remained among the treasures of the Royal Household. Craftsman Johann Christoph Bayer copied the delicate flower designs from the 51-volume botanical work *Flora Danica* over a period of 12 years. No two pieces are alike.

Of the original 1,802-piece Flora Danica service, 1,530 have survived. Some are here in Frederiksborg, others in Rosenborg Slot (see p 20). Queen Margrethe uses the service on state occasions and the pattern remains in production today, still hand-painted from the prints in the *Flora Danica*. The service is sold in the Royal Copenhagen shop in Strøget, Copenhagen (see p 76).

images of Danish resistance heroes, and an arresting image of an elderly Karen Blixen (see p 21) dressed as a Pierrot.

5 ★★ **Baroque Gardens.** Revived in the 1990s according to original drawings, these delightful formal gardens stretch into the distance across the castle's moat. Four sections of box hedge are shaped into royal monograms; from there steps lead through new planting and lush lawns to a romantic expanse of ancient trees and Frederik II's folly

Bath House Castle, occasionally used by the Royal Family for hunting lunches.

6 ★★ **kids** Spisestedet **Leonora.** A family-orientated establishment serving up salads, roasts, fish dishes, and *smørrebrød* and on a winning streak as the only restaurant in the palace complex. There's a great terrace for sunny days (see p 102). *Frederiksborg Slot, Hillerød.* ☎ *+45 4826 7516. www.leonora. dk. $$.*

View of the formal gardens from the Castle.

Kronborg Slot, Helsingør

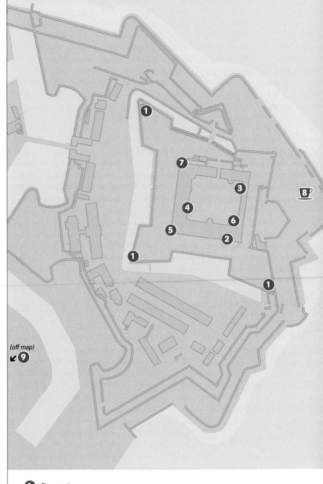

(off map)

1. Ramparts
2. Chapel
3. Royal Chambers
4. Danish Maritime Museum
5. Telegraph Tower
6. Ballroom and Little Hall
7. Casemates
8. Picnic
9. Helsingør

On a windswept headland on the northeast tip of North Zealand, majestic Renaissance Kronborg Slot (Castle) guards the entrance to the Øresund and looks out towards Sweden. The UNESCO World Heritage Site you see today was built in 1585 for Frederik II to ward off attack from the sea but a small castle existed here from the 1420s, built by Erik of Pomerania (see p 167). Notorious for William Shakespeare setting *Hamlet* in the castle, Kronborg is undergoing a long-overdue overhaul, slated to finish in summer 2010. The Danish Maritime Museum will move two years later. Make time to explore Helsingør after visiting the castle. START: **Driving from Copenhagen, take the E47 north to Helsingør; the journey is 46km and takes an hour. The S-train Line F from Hovedbanegården (Central Station) to Helsingør leaves every 20 minutes and takes 45 minutes. It's a 10-minute walk to the castle.**

❶ ★★ **kids** **Ramparts.** The imposing ramparts and fortified bastions of the castle were built by Christian V in 1690. Follow the informative history trail as it explains how Helsingør became rich under the rule of Erik of Pomerania through taxes levied on trading ships sailing up the Øresund. From the ramparts, cannons point seaward and you'll be awe-inspired by the massive bulk of northern Europe's biggest castle. Across sparkling blue seas, Helsinborg in Sweden is tantalizingly close at 4km away. The most romantic time to walk around these ramparts is at dusk in summer as the sun goes down.

❷ ★★★ **Chapel.** A lucky survivor of a fire in 1629 that saw much destruction at Kronborg, the chapel is opposite the main entrance off the vast cobbled courtyard. The decoration here serves as a reminder of how the castle once looked; ceilings and walls are wood paneled and gilded, the pulpit and private box in which the Royal Family attended Mass are ornately carved and brightly painted. Easily the most impressive part of the castle.

Kronborg Castle stands high over the moat and ramparts.

The ornate chapel.

③ ★ Royal Chambers. Found on the second floor, these rooms are sparsely furnished and bare-walled but have a certain austere splendor, if only for their size.

④ ★ kids Danish Maritime Museum. Housed at Kronborg since 1915, the second-floor Maritime Museum has Denmark's largest collection of naval artifacts and reflects the importance of the sea to this island state; an array of ephemera is squirreled away in a seemingly endless series of rooms. Unless you are fanatical about all things nautical, cherry pick your way through the prime exhibits, which include a delicate ivory model of a Chinese pleasure boat and 18th-century porcelain. Maps and charts explain Danish colonialism—you will come across a presentation on Jonas Bronk, who claimed 160 square miles of land in the New World in 1639 and founded the Bronx. Danish architects BIG won the competition to design the new museum, which is being built underground around an excavated dry dock in the castle grounds. Let's hope the exhibits match up to their smart new home when they move in spring 2012.

⑤ ★★ kids Telegraph Tower. At the end of the Maritime Museum, climb the spiral staircase to reach the flat-roofed tower for views up and down the coast. From here, signals were sent to Copenhagen in times of war; today, relentless streams of ferries pass by on their way to Sweden.

⑥ ★ Ballroom and Little Hall. At 62 x 12m, the largest hall in northern Europe was finished in 1585. The restoration hints at its former grandeur, with the magnificent marble floor and massive oil paintings adorning the walls. Tapestries in the Little Hall depict royal portraits, part of series commissioned by Frederik II in 1580.

⑦ ★★ Casemates. Dank, dark, and unsettling, these rambling dungeons have housed a thousand soldiers and their supplies for weeks in times of siege. Today they are enlivened by eerie contemporary art installations and a giant illuminated sculpture of Holger Danske, the mythical protector of Denmark. Legend goes that he sleeps in the casemates and will only awake to save his country when it is in mortal danger.

Practical Matters: Kronborg Castle

Ticket prices and combinations for **Kronborg Castle** vary from 85DKK (65DKK concessions; 25DKK kids 6–14), which allows access to the whole complex, to 30DKK (20DKK for children 6–14) to visit the Chapel and Casemates. During renovation work, various parts of the castle may be closed, but details were not available at the time of writing. Copenhagen Cards (see p 8) can be used for entrance to the Maritime Museum but not the castle. English-language guided tours start from the shop at 12.30pm and 2.30pm. *Kronborg 2c, 3000 Helsingør.* ☎ *+45 4921 3078. www.kronborgcastle.com.* Daily 10.30am–5pm. It will take approximately three hours to visit the castle, plus another three or four to look round town and the museums.

8 ★★ **Picnic** kids Buy picnic supplies and fresh fruit from the daily market in front of the Tourist Information Bureau in Havnepladsen and enjoy lunch in the castle grounds overlooking the sea. If you are in Helsingør at suppertime, head to **Peccati di Gola** for Sardinian pasta dishes (see p 102). *Kongensgade 6, Helsingør.* ☎ *+45 4929 8283. www. peccatidigola.dk.*

9 ★★★ **Helsingør.** This is a small, cheerful town with a cluster of half-timbered houses in a medieval quarter brimming over with tourists, and lots of bars, cafés and restaurants (see p 102 for my choice) overflowing onto cobbled streets. Two sandy beaches around the marina at

Nordhavn have shallow water and are safe for all the family; if the weather is poor, there is an indoor water park at the Hotel Marienlyst (see p 134). The **Bymuseum** of local history is in a medieval convent at Karmeliterhuset, Sankt Anna Gade 36, ☎ + 45 4928 1800, www.museerne.helsingor.dk. Admission 20DKK; 10DKK seniors; free kids under 18. Tues–Fri, Sun 12–4pm; Sat 12–2pm. The **Vinmuseum** (wine museum) in Helsingør's oldest wine cellar looks at the history of importing and bottling of wine. Strandgade 93, ☎ + 45 4921 0929, www.helsingorvinkompagni.dk. Admission free. Mon–Fri 10am–5.30pm, Sat 10am–2pm. The **Tourist Office** is at Havnepladsen 3, ☎ +45 4921 1333, www.visithelsingor.dk. Mon–Fri 10am–4pm. 🕐 3–4 hrs.

The spacious ballroom.

Malmö, Sweden

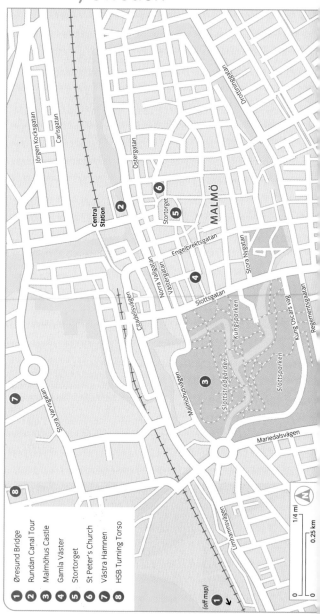

1. Øresund Bridge
2. Rundan Canal Tour
3. Malmöhus Castle
4. Gamla Väster
5. Stortorget
6. St Peter's Church
7. Västra Hamnen
8. HSB Turning Torso

ore than 18,000 commuters make their way across the Øresund Bridge daily from Malmö to Copenhagen; you can do it the other way around by taking the train to Sweden for the day. Malmö is a pleasant suburban city with an atmospheric old town packed with castles, churches, museums, and cafés juxtaposed with a burgeoning docklands area, its very own skyscraper, and sandy beaches. There's plenty to do and see within walking distance. START: The S-train from Hovedbanegården (Central Station) to Malmö departs every 20 minutes and the journey takes 35 minutes. The Gråhundbus line 999 leaves Rådhuspladsen once an hour and the journey takes 70 minutes. If you travel by car, the toll on the Øresund Bridge is 260DKK *each way*—it's sensible to take the train or the bus.

❶ ★★★ kids **Øresund Bridge.** Connecting Denmark with Sweden, the photogenic Øresund Bridge stretches across the water by bridge and tunnel and is both a rail and road bridge. Trains decant into Malmö city center and the tourist office is in the station. By 2011, a tunnel will have been completed connecting the station to the bridge. ⏱ 40 min from Copenhagen, 10 min to cross bridge.

❷ ★★ kids **Rundan Canal Tour.** Get your bearings with a boat trip along the canals that encircle Malmö's old town. Embarkation is at the boathouse outside the station and commentary is in English. The route skirts the Western Docks, where new buildings are going up at an astounding rate, before passing through the grounds of **Malmöhus**

Castle, and chugging under a sequence of low bridges. If you order in advance, the boat can put together a picnic for your round trip. ⏱ *45 min.*

❸ ★★ **Malmöhus Castle.** Turn right out of the station and walk for five minutes until you reach Malmö's 16th-century castle, built by the Danish monarch Christian III when the city belonged to Denmark. As at Kronborg Castle (see p 146), Erik of Pomerania built the original citadel in 1434. Part of the castle is now a museum with well-preserved Renaissance interiors; the modern section houses an art museum and aquarium. ⏱ *1½ hr. Malmöhusvägen.* ☎ *+46 040 34 4437. Admission 40SEK; 10SEK children 7–15. Sept–May daily 12pm–4pm; June–Aug daily 10am–4pm.*

Practical Matters: Malmö

Malmö Tourist Information Centre: Central Station, S-211 20 Malmö, Sweden. ☎ +46 4034 1200. The Malmö Card works like the Copenhagen Card (see p 8), permitting free transport and entrance to the museums; pick a one-day card up at the tourist office for 130SEK, which is currently about 98DKK. Canal trips (Rundan, ☎ +46 40 611 7488) are joined at the boathouse outside the station.

The vast font at St Peter's Church.

4 ★★ **Gamla Väster.** Across Slottsgatan and like a miniature Prague (or Buda in Budapest), the narrow cobbled streets and piazzas of Malmö's pedestrianized medieval core are lined with brightly painted houses and a bohemian air prevails in the buzzing bars and cafés. Contemporary art galleries and expensive boutiques add to the mix. The

little square of Lilla Torget is a charming place to lunch; on sunny days tables spread out across the cobbles under colored umbrellas. ⏱ *30 min.*

5 ★★ **Stortorget.** Lying almost next to Lilla Torget and surrounded by Gothic and Dutch Renaissance civic buildings, this square is at the heart of medieval Malmö. It is dominated by the massive façade of the Rådhuset (city hall), built in 1546 and reworked in Dutch Renaissance style in the 1860s. Close by, a copper King Karl X Gustav peers snootily from his vast equestrian perch; it was he who pulled back Malmö from its Danish conquerors in 1658 (see p 167). ⏱ *15 min.*

6 ★★ **St Peter's Church.** A step away from Stortorget, this cavernous church is Malmö's oldest building, dating from the early 14th century and constructed in what is known locally as Baltic Brick Gothic. Severe and suitably pinnacled on the outside, inside it is vividly white. The massive stone pulpit and the

Rådhuset in Stortorget, the symbol of civic pride.

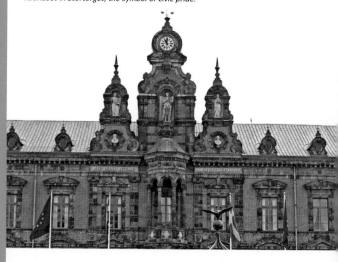

great gilt altar are fancifully elaborate in Renaissance style. My favorite corner of the church is the Kramarkapellet, a little chapel, with faded frescoes of dancing demons on the walls. ⏱ *45 min. Göran Olsgatan.* ☎ *+46 0435 296 80. Free admission. Mon–Fri 8am–6pm; Sat 9am–6pm; Sun 10am–6pm.*

❼ ★★ Västra Hamnen (Western Harbor). Across the harbor Sweden's answer to London's Docklands development is radically changing the face of waterside Malmö. Industrial degeneration is being rapidly replaced by smart apartment blocks, jazzy office buildings, trendy bars and cafés, amid a tangible sense of affluence and purpose. Things get lively by night, when a smartly dressed crowd bar-hops along the quays. ⏱ *1 hr.*

❽ ★★★ HSB Turning Torso. Spanish architect Santiago Calatrava's (designer of the dazzling Alamillo Bridge in Seville, Spain) twisting, turning creation stands out over the Western Docks. You'll spot it easily; as Sweden's tallest building, the tower stands 190 meters and is built in nine segments of five-story sections, which turn

Calatrava's twisted building dominates the skyline on the Western Harbor.

90 degrees from top to bottom. Most floors house luxury apartments and there is no access to the building, but you can take the virtual tour at the event center next door. It looks spectacular, especially when floodlit at night. ⏱ *30 min. Västra Varvsgatan 34.* ☎ *+46 4017 4500. Turning Torso Event Centre Västra Varvsgatan 44.* ☎ *+46 4017 4539.*

Øresund Bridge: The Facts

The bridge was opened on July 1 2000 by Queen Margrethe (see p 168) after five years of construction; its main span is 490m and the highest pillar stands at 204m. At 7.8km in length it has four road lanes and two rail tracks, which run underneath the road. Soaring halfway across the Øresund from the Swedish coastline to Peberholm, a man-made island 4km long, the road-and-rail bridge tunnels under the sea and resurfaces on Danish soil 4.5km later. Designers created the tunnel on the Danish side, as the bridge is close to Copenhagen airport, and the high spans were considered too dangerous to incoming aircraft.

Louisiana Museum

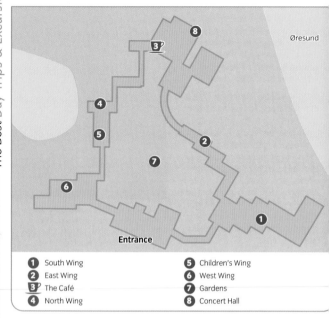

Øresund

Entrance

1 South Wing		**5** Children's Wing
2 East Wing		**6** West Wing
3 The Café		**7** Gardens
4 North Wing		**8** Concert Hall

A delight for art fiends, Louisiana is an extraordinary museum-cum-gallery straddling hilltop grounds between Copenhagen and Helsingør, with views sweeping across the Øresund. Designed as an adjunct to an aristocratic mansion built in 1855, the new galleries snake across the park, flowing from wing to wing. Since opening in 1958, there has been gradual expansion overseen by Danish architects Jørgen Bo and Vilhelm Wohlert. The whole trip from Copenhagen takes about 4 hours. START: It's a 35km drive from Copenhagen; take the E47 north and leave at junction 4, signposted Humlebæk, or drive along the coast road (152) and Louisiana is signposted on the right. The S-train Line F from Hovedbanegården (Central Station) to Humlebæk departs every 20 minutes and the journey takes 35 minutes. From there, it's a good 15-minute walk to the museum.

1 ★★★ **kids** **South Wing.** On entering the gallery through the main doors of the old house, turn right to discover minimalist spaces exhibiting vast artworks from the permanent collection. A few steps in and you can see a Rietveld *Red/Blue Chair* from 1918, the spectacular *Spider Couple* by Louise Bourgeois (1911–), and an electrifying *Ctesiphon II*, painted by Frank Stella (1936–) in 1967. The curious *Half Circle* by Spanish installation artist Juan Moñoz (1953–2001)

Country house and gallery at Louisiana.

attracts lots of attention from kids, who adore the gurning faces on the half-sized figures portrayed in a gray-clad circle. A gallery at the top of the South Wing looks right over the Øresund and delights kids with a diving board pointing seaward.

2 ★★ **East Wing.** A sun-filled passage leads on to the East Wing, passing indigenous American artifacts and leading to temporary exhibitions. In 2009 a Max Ernst retrospective and photography exhibition is scheduled. Visit the website (*www.louisiana.dk*) for details of current and future shows.

3 ★★ **kids** **The Café.** With panoramic views across the sea and a summer terrace, the museum café serves pastries and a buffet throughout the day followed by Danish-influenced dishes at night. *Closes at 8.30pm. $$.*

4 ★★ **North Wing.** Featuring further works from the museum's own collection, the North Wing's highlights include drawings by Hockney and Picasso plus the lumpy *Lava Chair* by American sculptor Scott Burton (1939–1989). Seminal Danish

Practical Matters: Louisiana Museum of Modern Art

Admission to Louisiana costs 90DKK (80DKK concessions, children up to 18 go free). Copenhagen Cards (see p 8) are accepted. Opening hours are Tues–Fri 11am–10pm; Sat–Sun 11am–6pm, although the museum is open some Mondays during school vacations. Guided tours are available in English Tues–Fri 11am–10pm; book in advance on the website. *Gammel Strandvej 13, 3050 Humlebæk.* ☎ *+45 4919 0791. www.louisiana.dk.*

artist Asger Jorn (1914–1973), a major figure with the CoBrA Group, has a room devoted to his garishly distorted images. Spindly sculptures on display in the Giacometti Room look as though they are about to walk away.

5 ★★★ kids **Children's Wing.** Opening up the world of art for kids, this three-story block offers courses, group activities at the weekend, and the chance to experiment with paint and clay. There are family guided tours of important pieces in the museum. The computer room and story-telling room keep children absorbed.

6 ★★ **West Wing.** Added in 1971, this wing displays changing artworks from the permanent collection. You might get to see American Pop Art from Andy Warhol or Roy Lichtenstein, or somber examples of German Expressionism by Georg Baselitz as well as mad sculptures by Jean Tinguely.

7 ★★ kids **Gardens.** Wander around rolling parkland and get up close to sculptures from Heerup and Moore. The Lake Garden showcases five different summerhouses by international architects. It's ideal for a summer's day, when children can let off steam in the open grounds.

8 ★★ **Concert Hall.** Has a yearly program of classical and jazz concerts. See the website for details. ●

The
Savvy Traveler

Before You Go

Government Tourist Offices

In the US: 655 Third Avenue, 18th Floor, New York, NY 10017 (☎ 212/885 9700, www.visitdenmark.com), or PO Box 4649, Grand Central Station, New York, NY 10063. **In the UK:** 55 Sloane St, London SW1X 9SY (☎ 020 7259 5959, www.visit denmark.com). **In Australia:** Level 4, 81 York Street Sydney, NSW 2000 (☎ 2/9262 5832, www.visitdenmark. com).

The Best Time to Go

It's always the right time to go to Copenhagen. The **spring** months are cool but often sunny; **May** through to **September** are the warmest months with long and balmy nights but the most rainfall and the most visitors. A visit in the **winter** will find a quieter city but the chance to skate on Kongens Nytorv (see p 85) and huddle under blankets by the heaters in the pavement cafés. Tivoli at Christmas is a rare treat for children, with visits from Santa and a festive market. Prices in the hotels may also be slightly lower in the winter months, with the exception of the weeks around Christmas and New Year.

Festivals & Special Events

SPRING. The **Night Film Festival** (late March, www.natfilm.dk) is held in Copenhagen and four other Danish cities, featuring obscure international films, new Danish releases, old classics, and cult films. The **Wednesday Concerts** (www. onsdagskoncerter.dk) held Wednesdays throughout spring and autumn are mainly classical. Free performances are given by students of the Royal Danish Academy of Music at the university, in the Theatre Museum (see p 39), and in churches across Copenhagen.

SUMMER. **Copenhagen Architecture Design Days (Cph ADD)** (mid May, www.cphadd.com) celebrates the city's architecture and design with a series of guided walks, lectures, workshops, and an international furniture fair in Bella Center. **Copenhagen Distortion** (June, www.cphdistortion.dk) is the best clubbing event of the year; a massive five-day party with lots of improvisation, special club nights, and late-night frolics. July is the month when things really hot up in Copenhagen. The **Copenhagen Jazz Festival** (early July, www. festival.jazz.dk) kicks things off when international jazz musicians hit town to perform in a series of around 450 (mostly free) concerts in squares, parks, cafés, bars, and late-night clubs. Dizzy Gillespie, Sonny Rollins, Herbie Hancock, and Oscar Peterson have all played. The most famous festival in Denmark is the huge **Roskilde Festival** (early July, www.roskilde-festival.dk), now up there with the biggest rock events in the world. Held in the countryside outside Roskilde, over 90,000 music fans pour in annually to see big-name and indie artists and to enjoy the hundreds of stalls, theater, acrobatics, bars, cyber cafés, and dance tents. Later in July, Santa Clauses from all over the world tip up at Bakken Amusement Park (see p 36) for the annual **Father Christmas Congress** (www.bakken.dk), with lots of fun and games for kids. **Cultural** Harbor (August, www. kulturhavn.dk) is a yearly jamboree around the harbor, with four days of cultural and leisure events, all for free.

Up north in Helsingør, the outdoor courtyard of Kronborg Castle (see p 146, www.hamletsommer.dk)

features a summer-long celebration of the works of Shakespeare and other playwrights. Back in Copenhagen, the first Saturday in August sees a huge concert (www.kglteater.dk) in the Fælledparken (see p 68) starring the Royal Opera soloists and orchestra. During **Copenhagen Summerdance** (August, www.copenhagensummerdance.dk), Tim Rushton and the Danish Dance Theatre (see p 118) perform outdoor shows in the courtyard of the Copenhagen City Police HQ. This is followed by **Copenhagen's Ballet Festival** (third week August, www.copenhageninternationalballet.com) of classical and modern dance, showcasing contemporary choreographers. The founder Alexander Kølpin works with dancers from all over the world. Gourmets convene in Tivoli and selected restaurants around town for the annual Nordic Food and Drink Festival, **Copenhagen Cooking** (August–September, www.copenhagencooking.com).

FALL. **Golden Days** in Copenhagen (September, www.goldendays.dk) aims to augment historical awareness through music, theatre, ballet, and literature. Copenhagen International Film Festival (CIFF) (end September, www.copenhagenfilmfestival.com) is a week-long celebration of outstanding Danish directors such as Lars von Trier, Thomas Vinterberg, and Søren Kragh-Jacobsen. An international jury judges the main competition. **Copenhagen Gay & Lesbian Film Festival** (CGLFF, October, www.cglff.dk) is the oldest film festival in town. For the past 17 years, the festival has become a fixture in the gay and lesbian subculture of Copenhagen, but is becoming increasingly mainstream. The following month, **CPH: DOX** (November, www.cphdox.dk) presents new and innovative documentaries, directors' Q&A sessions,

lectures along with music and club events.

WINTER. The Irish Festival arrives in the city in November with main concerts held in the old union hall at the Arbejdermuseet (see p 67) alongside smaller sessions held at venues around town (see www.irishfestival.dk for full line up and venue information). Santa **Claus's arrival at Tivoli** occurs in December amid much sparkle following on from the opening of **'Christmas in Tivoli'** (Nov–Dec, www.tivoli.dk), where the Christmas lights are designed by Tiffany's head designer. At the start of the new year, countrywide Jazz Festival **Vinterjazz** (Jan–Feb, www.vinterjazz.dk) holds events in Copenhagen's Operaen (see p 119). New fashion trends are showcased at the **International Fashion Fair** in February (www.ciff.dk), coinciding with the winter edition of **Copenhagen Fashion Week** (www.copenhagenfashionweek.co).

The Weather

Denmark has a moderate maritime climate with reasonably mild weather; but expect gray skies and some cold snaps, frost, and occasional snow during in December and January. Even so, temperatures rarely fall below -1°C due to Copenhagen's proximity to the sea's warming influence. In summer the mercury can get up as high as 25°C, with average temperatures around 20–21°C. Rainfall in Copenhagen is heaviest during the summer months, with up to 74mm in July. Due to its northern latitude, days are short in winter with about five hours of daylight in December and January. This of course is compensated for in the summer, with up to 18 hours of daylight, making May through October the pleasantest time to visit the city. The sea is warm enough to swim in by July, and if you wrap up well, the clear

COPENHAGEN'S AVERAGE TEMPERATURE & RAINFALL

AV RAINFALL	MM	INCHES	AV TEMP	°F	°C
Jan	43	1.7	Jan	32	0
Feb	25	1.0	Feb	32	0
Mar	36	1.4	Mar	35	2
Apr	41	1.6	Apr	44	7
May	41	1.6	May	53	12
June	53	2.1	June	60	16
July	66	2.6	July	64	18
Aug	74	2.9	Aug	63	17
Sept	51	2.0	Sept	57	14
Oct	53	2.1	Oct	49	9
Nov	53	2.1	Nov	42	6
Dec	51	2.0	Dec	37	3
Total	587	23			

skies and frosts of a sunny winter's day can be a real treat.

Cell (Mobile) Phones

Most UK and European phones can send and receive calls/SMS on international roaming in Copenhagen. Most GSM (Global System for Mobiles) tri-band cell phones from the US will also work. Call your wireless operator and ask for 'international roaming' to be activated or make sure the facility is triggered when you purchase your cell phone.

Useful Websites

All the website given below have English content.

www.copenhagen.com: Online version of the English-speaking weekly listings magazine, with up-to-the-minute news on shopping, nightlife, sport and so on.

www.copenhagenet.dk: A succinct history of Copenhagen plus a look at some of its main attractions and an events calendar.

www.goscandinavia.com: Official site of the Scandinavian tourist authorities; good for map, sightseeing information, and ferry schedules before you go.

www.hotels-in-denmark.dk: A one-stop hotel booking service, with details of accommodation throughout Denmark.

www.rejseplanen.dk: Find your way around Copenhagen's public transport system with ease.

www.visitdenmark.com: Official site of the Danish Tourist Board; good for maps of areas outside Copenhagen and itineraries.

www.visitcopenhagen.com: The superb official site of Wonderful Copenhagen. Very helpful on all aspects of a visit from nightlife to hiring bikes and buying discount passes. Information constantly updated.

But be warned—roaming charges can be high for texting and making calls. Cell phone reception is generally good in Copenhagen.

Rent **Nokia** or **Motorola** GSM mobiles in Copenhagen for around 175DKK per week; try the kiosks at Kastrup Airport. If you are staying for any length of time, it may be cheaper to buy a pay-as-you-go mobile phone package or SIM card rather than renting a handset. Try **Telia** (telia.dk), **TDC** (tdc.dk), or **Sonofon** (www.sonofon.dk). You can order a Danish SIM card on line from **Lebara** (www.lebara.dk) if you have a Danish contact address. North Americans can rent a GSM phone before leaving home from **InTouch USA** (☎ 800/872-7626; www.intouchglobal.com) or **Road-Post** (☎ 888/290-1606 or 905/272-5665; www.roadpost.com).

Car Rentals

Driving in Copenhagen isn't really necessary; the city is compact and the public-transport system works punctually as well as being free to Copenhagen Card holders (see p 8). Even outside the city, it is possible to get to all the tourist attractions (such as Hillerød, Helsingør, and Roskilde) by train. However, a car permits greater freedom when exploring the countryside, so hiring one for a few days is a consideration. The world's major car-rental companies, including **Avis** (www.avis.com), **Budget** (www.budget.com), **Europcar**, and **Hertz** (www.hertz.com), all have offices in Copenhagen as well as at Kastrup Airport and Hovedbanegården (Central Station). Significant savings can be made by booking online. **Sixt** (www.sixt.co.uk) and **Thrifty** (www.thrifty.co.uk) often have good deals if you book well in advance.

Getting There

By Plane

All travelers, whether coming from the US, Australia, or Europe, land at the one airport. After arrival at Copenhagen's Kastrup Airport (☎ +45 3231 3231, 12km from the city center), there are several ways to get into town. **Air-rail trains** (www.dsb.dk) link the airport with Hovedbanegården (Central Station) in 12 minutes. Fares are 28.50 DKK and the Air Rail Terminal is under the arrivals hall, an escalator ride from the gates. Trains depart every 20 minutes from four minutes past the hour. **Buses** 30, 250S, and 500S (www.movia.dk) depart regularly from outside arrivals to the city center; fares are 28.50DKK and the journey takes 30 minutes.

The **Metro** M2 line (yellow, www.m.dk) leaves every 4–6 minutes from the Air Rail Terminal and is an easy 15-minute journey into Kongens Nytorv; tickets cost 28.50DKK and the service runs between 5am and 12am Mon–Wed, 24-hours for the rest of the week. **Licensed taxis** wait outside the arrivals hall; fares into Copenhagen are about 200DKK and journey time is 25 minutes and upwards, depending on time of day.

By Car

European travelers choosing to drive to Copenhagen through Germany should catch a ferry to Gedser from Travemünde, and follow the E55 highway straight into the southern outskirts of the city. Coming from Sweden across the Øresund

Bridge brings drivers into the city past the airport on the E20.

By Bus

Buses from the surrounding areas in Zealand pull in at the Rådhuspladsen terminal (☎ +45 3613 1415), as do the services that run from Malmö in Sweden across the Øresund Bridge (see p 151). Rådhuspladsen is a two-minute stroll from the main railway station.

By Train

Run by **DSB** (www.dsb.dk), trains arrive at Hovedbanegården (Central Station, ☎ +45 7013 1415), right in the heart of the city. From here the local **S-Tog** trains depart to various destinations across Zealand, others to Funen, Odense, and Arhus. Taxis wait outside the main entrance to the station, and buses run from Rådhuspladsen, an easy few minutes' walk from the station. As the city is so compact, it may be possible to walk to your destination from the station; pick up a map from the information desk by track 5.

Note: neither Metro line connects to the main train station Hovedbanegården. If you want to pick up the Metro, it is best to stop at Nørreport station.

Getting Around

By Boat

The **Movia** harbor bus services 901, 902, and 903 (www.movia.dk) are a fun way to travel and useful when out sightseeing as they connect Den Sorte Diamond (Black Diamond, see p 30) with stops at Knippelsbro for Christianshavn, Nyhavn, and Holmen Nord for the Operaen (see p 119). Boats run every 10 minutes and the trip takes 20 minutes.

By Bike

Do as the locals do and whiz safely around town by bike, using the cycle lanes and backstreets. See p 85 for hire details. Free bikes are available all over town for a small deposit; for details see p 85.

By Bus

Tickets bought for any of the public-transport systems can be used on Metro, bus, and train. A basic ticket on the yellow Movia buses costs 20DKK and allows an hour's journey and unlimited transfers within your zone. Alternatively the 10-ride multi-ticket (*klippekort*) for zones one and two are useful for tourists, at 125DKK. An interesting route for visitors is service no. 29, which runs past Christiansborg (see p 39), Kongens Nytorv, Amalienborg (see p 15), and up to Langelinie (see p 17). Buses run from 5.30am to 12.30am daily, with night buses, (denoted by the 'N' after the route number), running into the suburbs from Rådhus-pladsen late into the night (as with trains, tariffs double during these hours).

By Car

As already mentioned in this section, there is little need for a car in Copenhagen unless you are planning to explore further in Zealand; parking is expensive and spaces are elusive. Expect to pay upwards of 25DKK per hour; the new blue parking meters take credit cards but most don't yet, so make sure you have 20DKK coins to feed the meter. Some hotels have private parking but nearly all charge for the facility.

By Metro

The **Metro** (☎ +45 7015 1615, www.m.dk) is driverless, modern, and reliable, running every two minutes during rush hours and every 15 minutes at night. Kongens Nytorv, Nørreport (which connects with local S-Tog trains), Vesterport, and Christianshavn are the most useful for tourists of the 23 stops along the two lines. Tickets can be bought from machines in all the Metro stations but the most sensible way to journey is to purchase a Copenhagen Card, which allows free travel (p 8). If buying tickets at the station, two children under 12 can travel free with each adult, a single-ride two-zone ticket is 20DKK or a two-zone multi-ride ticket with ten rides (klippekort) is 125DKK—make sure you clip them at the machines before you start your journey, and remember that tariffs double between 1am–5am Thur–Sun. Tickets for zones 1–3 are valid for an hour, tickets for all other zones for two, and are valid on all Metro trains, buses and S-Tog (local trains). Note: neither Metro line goes to the main train station Hovedbanegården. If you want to get to the main train station, take the Metro to Nørreport and take the S-Tog.

By Taxi

Taxis congregate around tourist attractions, notably Tivoli, Kongens Nytorv, Nyhavn, and Rådhuspladsen, as well as outside the airport and Central Station. In other places, cabs can be hailed if their light is showing the word 'fri'. Most taxi drivers speak some English and the meter should be started when you get in; fares are fixed at a price per km. Round up the tip to the nearest kroner or add 10DKK if paying by credit card. Drivers will produce a receipt on demand. Rickshaw taxis also circle the city, especially around Nyhvan; be prepared to haggle over the price!

On Foot

Strolling in Copenhagen's pedestrianized heart is a pleasure and a must-do, as is exploring the gardens and parks and rambling paths along the canalsides. However, on major roads, pay close attention to the lights at pelican and zebra crossings, and don't attempt to jaywalk under any circumstances (it is illegal); car drivers simply do not slow down and seem to enjoy hooting and flashing their lights as they zoom past your toes.

Fast Facts

APARTMENT RENTALS Among the options are: Citi let (☎ +45 7022 2129, www.citilet.dk, see p 129), and high-end **Charlottehaven Serviced Apartments** (☎ +45 3527 1500. www.charlottehaven.com) catering for couples or business travelers. Apartments and penthouses are kitted out with fully functioning offices and the best-possible-taste kitchens and bathrooms. The spa is a bonus too.

ATMS/CASHPOINTS Most banks offer 24-hour ATMs. Maestro, Cirrus, and Visa cards are readily accepted at all ATMs. Change currency either at banks or at exchanges around the tourist areas of Rådhuspladsen and Strøget. Central Station's money exchange is open 8am–8pm daily. Automatic exchange machines are available at Jyske Bank, Vesterbrogade 5; Den Danske Bank, Vesterbrogade 9; and three branches of Unibank at Axelborg Plads.

BUSINESS HOURS   Banks are open Monday through Friday from 9.30am to 4pm (Thur 6pm).

CREDIT CARDS   Call credit-card companies when you discover your wallet has been lost or stolen and file a report at the nearest police precinct. Your credit-card company or insurer will require a police report number or record. **Visa's** US emergency number is ☎ 800/847-2911, or ☎ 0800 89 1725 in the UK (www.visa.com). **American Express** (www.amex. com) cardholders and traveler's check holders should call ☎ 800/ 221-7282 in the US, or ☎ +44 (0)1273 696 933 in the UK. **Master-Card** (www.mastercard.com) holders should call ☎ 800/307-7309 in the US, or ☎ 0800 96 4767 in the UK.

Warning   Take care when paying by credit card; all major venues and restaurants should now utilize the chip-and-pin system; question anyone who wants to take your card away to make payment to avoid the risk of card fraud and cloning. In addition, overseas credit cards attract a 3–5% surcharge on many restaurant bills.

DOCTORS   Are on call in case of emergency on weekdays 4pm–8am (☎ +45 7013 0041). Visits cost from 250DKK. EU citizens are not charged if they have an EHIC card (see p 165).

ELECTRICITY   Hotels operate on 220 volts AC (50 or 60 cycles) with two-pin plugs. UK and US visitors will need to buy adaptors, readily available in all airport shops.

EMBASSIES   **Australian Embassy** Dampfærgevej 26, 2nd floor, 2100 Copenhagen (☎ + 45 7026 3676); **Canadian Embassy** Kristen Bernikowsgade 1, 1105 Copenhagen (☎ +45 3348 3200); **UK Embassy** Kastelsvej 36–40, 2100 Copenhagen (☎ +45 3544 5200).

US Embassy Dag Hammarskjölds Allé 24, 2100 Copenhagen (☎ +45 3341 7100).

EMERGENCIES   For police, ambulance or fire service, dial ☎ 112; emergency calls from public phones are free.

GAY & LESBIAN TRAVELERS   Denmark has a liberal tradition towards homosexuality, being the first country in the world to recognize same-sex marriage in 1989, and since 1999 gay couples have been able to adopt the children of their partners. Various gay festivals take place throughout the year (see p 158) and there are many gay and lesbian clubs and bars in the city (see p 112). www.visit copenhagen.com/gayevents has lots of gay-specific information. www. copenhagen-gay-life.dk is another useful website with listings, transport, and cruising details.

HOLIDAYS   Holidays observed include: January 1 (New Year's Day); March/April (Maundy Thursday, Good Friday, and Easter Monday); April/May – 40 days after Easter (Day of Prayer); May 1 (May Day); May/June (Whit Monday); June 5 (Constitution Day); December 25 (Christmas); and December 26 (Feast of St Stephen).

INSURANCE   Check your existing insurance policies before you buy travel insurance to cover trip cancellation, lost luggage, medical expenses or car rental insurance. For more information, contact one of the following recommended insurers: **Access America** (☎ 866/ 807-3982; www.accessamerica. com); **Travel Guard International** (☎ 800/826-4919; www.travel guard.com); **Travel Insured International** (☎ 800/243-3174; www. travelinsured.com); and **Travelex Insurance Services** (☎ 888/457-4602; www.travelex-insurance.com). For travel overseas, most US health plans (including Medicare and

Medicaid) do not provide coverage, and the ones that do often require payment for services upfront. If you require additional medical insurance, try **MEDEX Assistance** (☎ 410/453-6300; www.medex assist.com) or **Travel Assistance International** (☎ 800/821-2828; www.travelassistance.com); for general information on services, call the company's Worldwide Assistance Services, Inc. at ☎ 800/777-8710.

European travelers can apply for an **EHIC** card (pick up an application form from main post offices or apply online at www.ehic.org.uk). This lasts 3–5 years and entitles holders to reduced or free emergency healthcare across the European Economic Area.

INTERNET Internet access is plentiful, both in cybercafés and hotels, most of which now offer Wi-Fi access. Two central locations are **DropZone** (Frederiksborggade 41, ☎ +45 3393 6888, www.drop-zone. dk) or **Boomtown** (Axeltorv 1, ☎ +45 3332 1032, www.boomtown. net). Mac users seek out **Verde Food and Coffee** (Nørre Farimags-gade 72, ☎ +45 7020 3015, Verde.dk, see p 80).

LOST PROPERTY The main lost-property office is in the police station at 113 Slotsherrensvej, 2720 Vanløse, ☎ +45 3874 8822. If you lose something on the train, call ☎ +45 3614 1701.

MAIL & POSTAGE Most post offices are open Monday–Friday about 9am–5pm and Saturday 9am–12pm. Closed Sunday. Mail boxes are bright red. Post offices in tourist areas are open longer hours and some open Sunday. Main branches are at Central Station (25–39 Tietgensgade), and 33 Købmagergade.

MONEY The currency in Denmark is the **krone**. At press time, the exchange rate was approximately

1DKK = [$]0.20 (or [£]0.12). For up-to-the minute exchange rates between the euro and the dollar, check the currency converter website **www.xe.com**.

OPENING HOURS Stores open Monday–Friday 9.30am–5.30–6.30pm and various hours on Sunday although, surprisingly, many close then, especially outside Copenhagen. Within Copenhagen, shops are allowed to open 23 Sundays per year (see p 82). Off licenses, kiosks, and the shops around Rådhuspladsen stay open until late at night.

PASSPORTS No visas are required for Australian, US, Canadian, or UK visitors to Denmark providing your stay does not exceed 90 days. If your passport is lost or stolen, contact your country's embassy or consulate immediately. See 'Embassies' above. Make a copy of your passport's critical pages and keep it separate from your passport.

PHARMACIES Pharmacies (apotek) have an illuminated 'A' outside and operate during normal business hours (see p 82). A 24-hour pharmacy is found at **Steno Apotek**, Vesterbrogade 6C (☎ +45 3314 8266, www.stenoapotek.dk) opposite Central Station.

POLICE The national police emergency number is ☎ 112.

RESTROOMS Toiletter or WC are available in most tourist areas of Copenhagen. Mens' facilities are marked as 'Herrer' or 'H', womens' as 'Damer' or 'D'. It is also not unusual to find unisex toilets in Denmark, even in public buildings.

SAFETY Denmark is one of the safest countries in Europe and violent crime in Copenhagen is extremely rare. However, take care around the Central Station at night; muggings have been known, mainly by the junkies who hang around the old Red Light District at the back of the station.

SMOKING   Smoking was banned in all indoor public places in August 2007. This ban covers public transport and the interiors of restaurants, bars, and cafés.

TAXES   The value-added (VAT) tax (known in Denmark as *moms*) hits in at 25%. This is included in the displayed price.

If you are traveling from outside the EU, you can obtain a tax rebate on purchases over 300DKK as you leave the country. Global Refund and Euro Refund offer 13–19% of your purchase price back. Shop where you see their sign and ask for a tax-free refund form at the till. Show your purchases, receipts, and passport at customs and the company will refund your money straight into your bank account. For more information, go to www.globalrefund.com or eurorefund.com.

TELEPHONES   The country code is **45**; there are no city codes in Denmark. Local numbers have eight digits. Pay phones accept 1DKK or 5DKK coins and pre-paid Telecards, available from kiosks and post offices (see p 165). For national telephone enquiries, dial ☎ **118**. For international telephone information, call ☎ **113**. For collect international calls, ☎ **141** for the operator. Be aware that these calls are charged at 5DKK per call, with an additional fee of 7DKK per minute.

International codes are: UK +44; US +1; Australia +61.

TIPPING   Round up taxi fares to the nearest krone. Service charges are built into most bills in restaurants; always check the bill before you leave a tip.

TOURIST INFORMATION   The excellent **Wonderful Copenhagen** (Gammel Kongevej 1, ☎ +45 3325 7400, www.visitcopenhagen.com) and **Copenhagen Right Now** (Vesterbrogade 4A, ☎ +45 7022 2442, www.woco.dk) tourist information offices are open seven days a week in the summer months, closed Sunday over winter.

TRAVELERS WITH DISABILITIES   Denmark is forward-thinking; all new public buildings are wheel-chair accessible, as are most of the museums, restaurants, larger shops, and the airport. Contact the **Danish Disability Council** (www.dch.dk) for details. For British travelers, the **Royal Association for Disability and Rehabilitation** (www.radar.org.uk) provides tips for planning holidays overseas. US citizens can contact the Society for Accessible Travel and Hospitality (www.sath.org) for travel hints and recommendations. **Flying Wheels Travel** (www.flyingwheelstravel.com) offers escorted tours and **Access-Able Travel Source** (www.access-able.com) has access information for people traveling to Copenhagen.

Copenhagen: A Brief History

810 First recorded Danish king, Godfred, dies.

800–950 Vikings plunder England, Russia, and France.

940–985 Harald Bluetooth brings Christianity to Denmark.

1013–43 England and Denmark united.

1160–67 Fortress built on the isle of Slotsholmen by Bishop Absalon to protect the new settlement of Copenhagen.

1240–1400 Rapid growth of the city due to its position on natural harbor of the Øresund.

1254 Copenhagen given a charter as a city by Bishop Jakob Erlandsen.

1369 Absalon's fortress razed to the ground by the German Hanseatic League.

1397 Queen Margrethe I (1353-1412) founded the Northern Alliance between Denmark, Norway, and Sweden, formalized as the Union of Kalmar.

1410 First Copenhagen Castle built on site of present Christiansborg Palace.

1417 King Erik of Pomerania first resident of castle.

1443 Copenhagen replaces Roskilde as Danish capital.

1449 King Christian I, the first of the Oldenborg dynasty, crowned in Copenhagen.

1471 Sweden breaks away from Union of Kalmar.

1479 University of Copenhagen founded by Christian I.

1536 Lutheran preachers bring Reformation to Denmark.

1583 The world's oldest amusement park established at Bakken.

1588–1648 Reign of principle architect of Copenhagen, Christian IV. Canals, Rosenborg Castle, Børsen, Kastellet, and Rundetårn built.

1658 The Peace of Roskilde hands Malmö back to the Swedes.

1675–79 Skåne Wars in which Denmark lost territory to Sweden.

1700–1810 City grows in wealth due to taxing of maritime traffic through the Øresund.

1711 Bubonic plague wiped out third of Copenhagen's population.

1728 Much of the city destroyed by fire.

1731–37 City rebuilt under Christian VI, including Copenhagen Castle, which became Christiansborg Palace.

1746–66 Frederiksstad and Amalienborg developed under Frederick V.

1775 Royal Porcelain Factory opened.

1794 Christian VI's palace at Christiansborg burned down. Royal Family moved to Amalienborg.

1801–07 British bombardment of Copenhagen, with heavy loss of life, to prevent Denmark siding with Napoleon.

1813 Denmark bankrupted after Napoleonic Wars. Ceded Norway to Sweden.

1810–30 Golden Age of Danish literature; luminaries were HC Andersen and Søren Kierkegård.

1814 First free compulsory primary schools.

1830–40 Copenhagen recovers from bankruptcy and extends beyond city walls to Vesterbro, Nørrebro, and Østerbro.

1843 Tivoli opened under auspices of Georg Carsten, friend of Andersen.

1847 Founding of Carlsberg Brewery. Central Station opened.

1849 Monarchy becomes constitutional; reforms signed in Copenhagen.

1863 House of Glücksborg succeeded the House of Oldenborg through King Christian IX (1863–1906).

1880 First wave of immigration to the US.

1890S A time of many liberal social reforms.

1914 Denmark retains neutrality during WWI.

1928 Third Christianborg Palace becomes seat of government.

1930S Economic depression.

1940–45 German occupation of Copenhagen during WWII.

1949 Denmark joins NATO.

1967 Copenhagen celebrates 800-year jubilee.

1972 Denmark joins EEC. Margrethe II becomes queen.

1992 Denmark votes against Mastricht Treaty.

1993 Accepts the Treaty and leads the European Union for six months.

1996 Cultural Capital of Europe.

2000 Øresund Bridge opened, connecting Denmark and Sweden.

2002 Metro opens.

2004 Operaen opens.

2005 Muhammed cartoons set off worldwide Muslim protests.

2008 Copenhagen is ranked as the best city in the world to live in.

Copenhagen's Architecture

Although the building of Copenhagen began in the 12th century with Bishop Absalon's fort on Slotsholmen (see p 19), much of what we see today is the result of the vision of the Royal Family. The present-day city began to take shape during the 52-year reign of Christian IV between 1596 and 1648.

17th-century Town Planning

Under the auspices of King Christian IV, many of the buildings we see today were built. As money and riches began to pour into the city, he went on a building spree only equalled by the development of the past 100 years. Rosenborg Castle, the Dutch Renaissance Børsen and the Rundetårn, complete with its observatory, all appeared during his reign, as did the canals to ease transport and the defensive walls of Kastellet.

18th-century Rococo

The Danish Royal Family live in their vast castle complex at **Amalienborg** in aristocratic Frederiksstaden, laid out 1746–1766

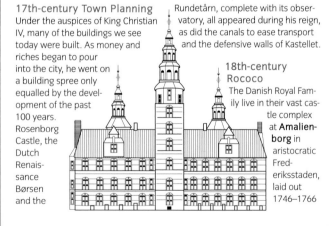

according to the visionary and ultimately over-ambitious plans of Frederik V. The castle's rococo-style buildings are some of the most impressive in northern Europe, offset by the waters of the Øresund and the domed majesty of the **Marmorkirken**. For further examples of Frederik's ambitions for his city, look no further than **Det Kongelige Teater**, with its arched balcony encrusted with mosaics, built at a time when Copenhagen was increasingly wealthy due to maritime trade and taxes.

19th-century Romanticism

Copenhagen's civic pride of the Golden Age is exemplified by the enormous **Rådhuset**, genius of architect Martin Nyrop and finished in 1906. He was inspired by the Palazzo Pubblico in Siena, wanting to create a building that dominated its surroundings with a massive tower and symbolic carvings, pinnacles and mini-turrets on all corners. A black-and-gilt figure of Bishop Absalon appears above the main entrance, meters away from the two symbolic *lur* (horn) players perched atop their giant brick pillar.

20th-century Modernism

The century of Arne Jacobsen, Georg Jensen, and Hans J. Wegner

(1914–2007). Jacobsen's Egg, Ant, and Swan chairs, Jensen's silverware, and Henningsen's lamp shades can be seen in hip bars, hotels, and museums throughout Copenhagen. Jacobsen is the godfather of Danish design and his greatest work is the **Radisson SAS Royal Hotel** (see p 132), Copenhagen's first skyscraper. The late 20th century was a time of great innovation in Copenhagen, as illustrated by the splendid French Wing at the **Ny Carlsberg Glyptotek** (see p 14). Designed by Henning Larsen and opened in 1996, it is masterly in its use of light and space. Two years later saw the opening of the magnificent glass-and-concrete extension to the **Nationalmuseet** by Anna Maria Indrio.

21st-century Minimalism

Ground-breaking contemporary designs include **Paustian**, the trend-setting furniture store and Michelin-starred restaurant in the docks (see p 93), designed by the architect of Sydney Opera House, Jørn Utzon (1918–2008). American wonderkid Daniel Libeskind designed the **Dansk Jødisk Museum** (see p 19) in 2004. Iraqi Zaha Hadid (b. 1950) worked the new wing of **Ordrupgaard Art Museum** (see p 31), which opened in 2005, and more recently Norman Foster got in on the act with the 2008 elephant house at the **Zoo** (see p 88). Although the current jewels in Copenhagen's architectural crown have to the

series of new public spaces, **Den Sorte Diamond** (Black Diamond, see p 30), the **Operaen** (see p 119), and **Det Kongelige Teater**

Skuespilhuset (Playhouse, see p 122), exciting buildings continue to appear with the redevelopment of Ørestad (see p 31).

Useful Phrases & Menu Terms

Useful Words & Phrases

ENGLISH	DANISH	PRONUNCIATION
Hello	Hej	hai
How are you?	Hvordan går det?	vaw-*dan gawr* day
Fine, thank you	Godt, tak	got tahk
What is your name?	Hvad hedder du?	vah *hith*-er doo
My name is...	Jeg hedder...	yigh *hith*-er
Where are you from?	Hvor kommer du fra?	*vohr komm*-er doo frah
How old are you?	Hvor gammel er du?	*vohr gahm*-el er doo
Thank you	Tak	tahk
Yes	Ja	yah
No	Nej	nay
Excuse me	Undskyld	*oon*-skewl
I'm sorry	Undskyld	*oon*-skewl
Goodbye	Farvel [formal] or Hej	fahr-*vell* or haj
Help!	Hjælp!	yelp
Good morning	Godmorgen	goh-*morn*
Good day	Goddag	goh-*day*
Good evening	Godaften	goh-*afden*
Good night	Godnat	goh-*naht*
I don't understand	Det forstår jeg ikke	day for-*stawr* yigh *igg*-ih
Do you speak English?	Taler du engelsk?	*teh*-ler doo *eng*-elsk
What time is it?	Hvad er klokken?	vah er *klok*-en
It's o'clock	Klokken er	*klok*-en er
morning	morgen	morn
afternoon	eftermiddag	*eft*-er-mih-*day*
evening	aften	*ahf*-den
night	nat	naht
noon	middag	mih-*day*
midnight	midnat	*mith*-naht
today	i dag	ee *day*
yesterday	i går	ee *gawr*
tomorrow	i morgen	ee *morn*
week	uge	*oo*-ih
Entrance	Indgang	*in*-gahng
Exit	Udgang	*ooth*-gahng
Open	Åben	*aw*-ben
Closed	Lukket	*loog*-et
Left	Venstre	*vehn*-strih
Right	Højre	*hoy*-rih

ENGLISH	DANISH	PRONUNCIATION
Police Station	Politistation	pol-ih-*tee*-stah-*shohn*
Police	Politiet	pol-ih-*tee*-it
Toilets	Toiletter	toy-*let*-er
Men	Herrer	*heh*-rer
Women	Damer	*dah*-mer
Tourist Information	Turistinformation	too-*reest*-in-for-mah-*shohn*
Post office	Posthus	*post*-hoos
Cathedral	Domkirke	*dom*-keerk-ih
Church	Kirke	*keerk*-ih
Main square	Torvet	*tor*-vit
Street	Gade/stræde	*gah*-thih
Castle	Slot	slot
Garden	Have	*hah*-vih
Square	Plads/torv	plahs/torv
Bookshop	Boghandel	*boh*-hand-ihl
Delicatessen	Delikatesse	dehl-ih-kah-*tess*-ih
Laundry	Vaskeri	vask-er-*ee*
Market	Marked	*mar*-kith
News agent	Aviskiosk	ah-*vees*-kee-osk

Numbers

NUMBER	DANISH	PRONUNCIATION
1	en (en)/et (ed)	En (ayn)/et (ayt)
2	to	toh
3	tre	tray
4	fire	fear
5	fem	fem
6	seks	seks
7	syv	sewh
8	otte	*awd*-ih
9	ni	nee
10	ti	tee
11	elleve	*ell*-vih
12	tolv	tawl
13	tretten	*trat*-en
14	fjorten	*fyort*-en
15	femten	*femt*-en
16	seksten	*sigh*-sten
17	sytten	*sewt*-en
18	atten	*aht*-en
19	nitten	*nitt*-en
20	tyve	*tew*-vih
21	enogtyve	ayn-oh-*tew*-vih
22	toogtyve	toh-oh-*tew*-vih
23	treogtyve	trey-oh-*tew*-vih
30	tredive	*trahll*-vih
40	fyrre	*fuhrr*
50	halvtreds	hal-*tres*
60	tres	tres

ENGLISH	DANISH	PRONUNCIATION
70	halvfjerds	hahl-*fyers*
80	firs	feers
90	halvfems	hahl-*fems*
100	hundrede	*hoon*-er
150	hundrede og halvtreds	*hoon*-er oh hahl-*tres*
200	to hundrede	toh *hoon*-er
300	tre hundrede	tray *hoon*-er
1000	tusind	*too*-sin
2000	to tusind	toh *too*-sin
1,000,000	en million abbr: en mio	ayn mil-ee-*ohn*

Days of the Week

ENGLISH	DANISH	PRONUNCIATION
Monday	mandag	*mahn*-dah
Tuesday	tirsdag	*teers*-dah
Wednesday	onsdag	*ohns*-dah
Thursday	torsdag	*tors*-dah
Friday	fredag	*frigh*-dah
Saturday	lørdag	*luhr*-dah
Sunday	søndag	*sewn*-dah

Months

ENGLISH	DANISH	PRONUNCIATION
January	januar	*yahn*-oo-ar
February	februar	*feb*-roo-ar
March	marts	mahrts
April	april	ab-*reel*
May	maj	migh
June	juni	*yoo*-nee
July	juli	*yoo*-lee
August	august	ow-*goost*
September	september	sept-*ehm*-ber
October	oktober	ok-*toh*-ber
November	november	noh-*vehm*-ber
December	december	days-*ehm*-ber

Menu Savvy

ENGLISH	DANISH	PRONUNCIATION
breakfast	morgenmad	*morn*-math
lunch	frokost	*froh*-kost
supper	aftensmad	*af*-dens-*math*
chicken	kylling	*kew*-ling
beef	oksekød	*oks*-e-*kewth*
fish	fisk	fisk
ham	skinke	*skin*-kih
cheese	ost	ohst
eggs	æg	eg
salad	salat	sa-*laht*
(fresh) vegetables	(friske) grøntsager	*frisk*-e *gruhnt*-say-er
(fresh) fruit	(frisk) frugt	frisk froogt

ENGLISH	DANISH	PRONUNCIATION
bread	brød	bruhth
toast	ristet brød	*rist*-et *bruhth*
noodles	nudler	*nood*-ler
rice	ris	rees
coffee	kaffe	*kah*-fih
tea	te	tay
juice	juice/saft	dyews/sahft
sparkling water	danskvand	*dansk*-vahn
water	vand	vahn
beer	øl	ool
red/white wine	rød/hvid vin	ruhth veen/vith veen
salt	salt	sahlt
black pepper	peber	*pay*-wuhr
butter	noget smør	*noh*-ith *smuhr*
May I have a glass of...?	Må jeg bede om et glas __?	maw yigh *bay*-thih om ayt glas
May I have a cup of ...?	Må jeg bede om en kop __?	maw yigh *bay*-thih om ayn kop
May I have a bottle of ...?	Må jeg bede om en flaske __?	maw yigh *bay*-thih om ayn flask
May I have some ...?	Må jeg bede om ___?	maw yigh *beh*-thih om
It was delicious	Det var lækkert.	day vahr *lek*-ert
Excuse me, waiter?	Undskyld! or Tjener!	*oon*-skewl or *tyeyn*-er
May I have the check, please	Må jeg bede om regningen?	maw yigh *bay*-thih om righ-ning-en

Photo Credits

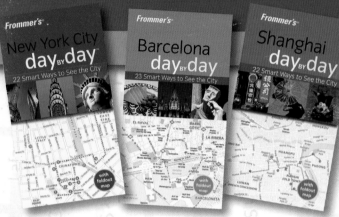